# PARTNERS

*[signature]*

DAVE FLYNN

**author**HOUSE

AuthorHouse™
1663 Liberty Drive
Bloomington, IN 47403
www.authorhouse.com
Phone: 833-262-8899

© 2023 Dave Flynn. All rights reserved.

No part of this book may be reproduced, stored in a retrieval system, or transmitted by any means without the written permission of the author.

Published by AuthorHouse  06/14/2023

ISBN: 979-8-8230-1012-2 (sc)
ISBN: 979-8-8230-1013-9 (hc)
ISBN: 979-8-8230-1014-6 (e)

Library of Congress Control Number: 2023911204

Print information available on the last page.

Any people depicted in stock imagery provided by Getty Images are models, and such images are being used for illustrative purposes only.
Certain stock imagery © Getty Images.

This book is printed on acid-free paper.

Because of the dynamic nature of the Internet, any web addresses or links contained in this book may have changed since publication and may no longer be valid. The views expressed in this work are solely those of the author and do not necessarily reflect the views of the publisher, and the publisher hereby disclaims any responsibility for them.

# Contents

Preface ................................................................................................ vii

Introduction ........................................................................................ ix

Chapter 1   In the Beginning ............................................................... 1

Chapter 2   In the Army Now .............................................................. 7

Chapter 3   Find a job ........................................................................ 13

Chapter 4   Got Married .................................................................... 19

Chapter 5   Buying a Home ............................................................... 23

Chapter 6   Made Dad a Partner ....................................................... 27

Chapter 7   Move to California ......................................................... 31

Chapter 8   Move back to Kentucky ................................................. 35

Chapter 9   Kenny Burger ................................................................. 37

Chapter 10  La Hacienda ................................................................... 43

Chapter 11  El Cabrito's ..................................................................... 47

Chapter 12  Nine Restaurants ........................................................... 51

Chapter 13  IRS .................................................................................. 53

Chapter 14  Carl Silver ...................................................................... 63

Chapter 15  Lupos and Hilltop Grocery ........................................... 67

Chapter 16  Family Restaurant ................................................................. 71

Chapter 17  Unemployment Commission ............................................... 75

Chapter 18  Change Sign .......................................................................... 79

Chapter 19  Bad Checks ............................................................................ 83

Chapter 20  Taxes ...................................................................................... 87

Chapter 21  Real Estate and Auctioneers License .................................. 91

Chapter 22  Contractors Class A Building License ............................... 93

Chapter 23  1985 ........................................................................................ 97

Chapter 24  Open 24 Hours ................................................................... 103

Chapter 25  Moved to Pantops ............................................................... 107

Chapter 26  Mr. Moore ............................................................................ 111

Chapter 27  Jackson ................................................................................. 113

Chapter 28  Pancake Franchise .............................................................. 121

Chapter 29  Gate Plaza ............................................................................ 125

Chapter 30  Chick-fil-A ........................................................................... 131

Conclusion ................................................................................................ 135

Epilogue ..................................................................................................... 139

# Preface

My name is Kati Forman. This story began for me on January 12, 2023. I was sitting in my doctor's office waiting to be seen. I was talking to God. Laying on the table. I got a text from a family friend "Sue." She asked if I would be interested in typing up a book by David Flynn. I said "possibly." I knew that God was in this story.

I was able to meet David and Katie Flynn on 1-20-23. I found out that their wedding anniversary is January 12$^{th}$. With God nothing is left to chance. I know that God is working. I feel so tiny in the presence of a majestic God. So unworthy. I do not know the beginning from the end, but He does. He knows all. He is the first and the last. The alpha and the omega.

I would love the opportunity to come along side this family. To listen to David's life story. To type his words down on paper, so that the next generation will know his feelings. I am honored for this position and I am overwhelmed at the same time. I know that my God will supply all my needs. His grace is sufficient for me.

Give me today my daily bread Lord, and thank you for this family. This marriage. This story. May you, Father God, get all the glory that you are due. In Jesus' name, Amen.

# Introduction

I am known for my stories. I can tell you thousands of stories. In this book, I have picked just a few of the ones that stand out to me, to try and get my point across. Thank you for reading it. I want everyone to take away from this book, the fact that we have partners in our lives from the time we are born, until the time we die. I was fortunate enough to have the Lord as one of my partners.

I also want to note, that as you read some of these stories, especially about my earthly father, I need you to know, that I loved him. As ornery as my dad was, he was my earthly father, and I was with him when he passed away. I have forgiven him, just as my Lord and savior God, has forgiven me. If it was not for the Lord, I do not know where I would be.

I believe in this life; you need three things to be successful. Education, drive, and common sense. If you at least have two of the three, you can get by okay, but it will be tough. If you have education and no common sense, life will be hard. If you have the education but no drive to work, that will be tough for you too. I was blessed enough to have some common sense. I was self-educated, meaning I learned my way through this life. I definitely had the drive to work, and earn a decent living. There is no such thing as a free lunch. Someone, somewhere, must pay for it. If you look at your paycheck, that has a deduction on it. When you buy gas, that has a tax on it. You do not have to be in business like I was, to be partnered with Uncle Sam. He is your partner from the moment you are born. No matter what walk in life you are in, you are contributing to that partner.

Thank you for taking this journey with me. May you have good partners in your life. Choose wisely.

David Flynn

# CHAPTER 1

# In the Beginning

IN THE BEGINNING THERE WAS GOD, NOT NOTHING; BECAUSE IF there was nothing, it would still be nothing. I have a lot of good stories to tell. What's great is that all my stories are true. So here we go. Let's get on with the program.

I am going to start at the beginning when I was born. I was born in 1940.

I was born in Boone County Kentucky. The house I was born in, was a little white house. It had no water. No electricity. The snow was deep. Mom had me in that house. The doctor couldn't get in and my dad didn't want to come in. He had been on a drinking binge and wasn't any help to my mother at that time. There was an African American lady who helped my mom out. If it hadn't been for her, I don't think mom or I would have made it. Mom had pneumonia. The next day the doctor was able to get in via horse. The snow was so deep, only a horse could make it. We both survived this little incident.

After that we moved to Hamilton Ohio. Dad couldn't get into the Army because he couldn't pass the medical test. It was either that he drank too much, or that he has gotten kicked by a cow. That was the story my dad told me anyway. He had a lot of stories himself.

When I was about 3 or 4 years old, my sister was about 8 or 9 years old. Mom worked at a factory and dad "ran the road." My sister would take me down to the corner bar and they would play this song, "I don't want her, you can have her, she's too fat for me". It was a popular song back then. They would play it on the juke box and I would tap dance on top of the bar. The guys would like it and throw nickels up to me. My sister would gather all that money and keep it for herself. I never did see that money. We did always have money for snacks though. We lived this way for a while.

Dad wanted to move back to Boone County Kentucky. That's where his mother was and she spoiled her son. That's probably why my dad acted the way he did. He was her baby boy and she always looked after him. She had a 180-acre farm and she gave him some money to build a house on it. We moved into that. That worked out pretty good for a while until I got a little older. When I was about 8 or 9, dad expected me to do everything that needed to be done. He'd hook the horses up and show me how to plow. I couldn't even pick the plow up. I had to lay the plow down at the end of the fur and drive the horses in a circle. Then I'd have to set it back up in order to plow, but I had to plow or else dad would whip by butt. This went on.

I was about 10. It didn't matter what I did, it was never good enough for him. If I could have left home at this age, I would have done it. One day I was hauling hay. One of the horses rubbed the bridal off of the other horse while they were eating. My cousin was throwing the hay up to the wagon to me. The horses started running away. I couldn't stop them because one didn't even have on a bridal. My cousin told me to jump off the wagon.

Like a dummy I did. I sprained my ankle really bad. The horses ran the wagon into the gate. Busted up the gate. The tongue of the wagon was busted too. I hobbled along enough to get the horses into the barn. My cousin and I made it to my mom. She took me to the doc. Doc gave me some crutches. Once dad got home, he wanted to know if we had gotten the hay up. I told him, "No we ran into some trouble with the horses". He was upset. "What kind of trouble?". Dad said "We're going to the barn". I was on crutches. Dad saw the gate. He saw the broken wagon tongue. He grabbed me by the arm. I lost my crutches. He whipped my butt and he whipped it good.

I could tell you lots of stories about my dad. He liked to drink. He drank a lot. He liked to beat me. He did it often. One day I was in the basement and I picked up a potato sprayer. I accidently sprayed it. When Dad got home, I got beat with the metal potato sprayer rod. He whipped me and he whipped me good. This went on for a while.

When I was about 13, I had saved some money and I had my own stock. Cows, rabbits, turkeys, ponies. It didn't matter how much I owned; my grandmother owned ½ of everything. I had a partnership with my grandmother. It was my first partnership. When we're born, we're born into a partnership. The government. There is also another partnership. The one you need, the Lord! That's the one you choose. At the age of 10, I chose the Lord. If it hadn't been for Him, I don't know how I would have gotten through my other partnership with the government. I've backslidden in my life but I did choose the Lord when I was 10. I'll get to more of those stories later on.

Back home on the farm, one time I had to kill a black snake because he was eating the chicken eggs. This was not something we normally did because the black snakes ate the mice. I cut off his head and threw him out in the hog pen. Daddy found him. He took the snake and beat me with it. My daddy was a piece of work. When I was 11, I had saved up 12 dollars in a mason jar. I wanted to buy a baby calf with it. Back then you could buy a calf for 9 dollars. My dad got the calf for me, but he kept the other 3 dollars for himself. He told me right then, that I had to learn in life I didn't get something for nothing. That's the kind of man my daddy was.

By the time I was 15, I had saved enough money to buy a car. A 1947 Pontiac convertible. One day my dad came home with a goat. That darn thing climbed all over my car. It jumped up onto the roof of that convertible and fell right through the top. Blasted thing! Goats aren't the smartest creatures.

As soon as I was 16, I was able to get a job at the grocery store. My dad didn't like this. He wanted me to stay and work on the farm doing what he wanted me to do and to whip me whenever he wanted to. By this age, I had gotten big enough that he couldn't beat me anymore. However, one time when I was 16, him and I got into it, outside in the snow. He knocked me down and got on top of me. He was holding my face down into the snow. Mom was screaming at him. I was able to grab a tool and knock him off of me. I wanted to hit him hard but mom told me, "No!"

One night I was going a little too fast in my Pontiac, and slid off into the ditch. My dad knew about it, but he wouldn't help me get my car out of that ditch. He told me that it could stay right there where it was. My dad and I had this type of relationship.

One day he had a box with all my clothes in it, and he told me to leave. I was more than happy to get out of there. I went to live with my grandmother. Soon after that my parents split up after 21 years. I didn't like the change of school I was in. The high school was too big. By 17 I told my mother I wanted to join the army. I was living with her at this point in my life. She said she would sign for me. I was ready to move onto the next chapter of my life. The army.

Thank you, Lord, for getting me through this part of my life.

# CHAPTER 2

# In the Army Now

On April the 21st 1957, I joined the Army. I went to Fort Knox, Kentucky for my basic training. You had to qualify with an M1 rifle. I was there for 8 weeks. You had to shoot at the target. Way down in the field. You had to hit the middle. I know that I hit the target the first time, but the guys training me wanted to mess with me. Instead of the target I had hit, they held up "Maggie's drawers" on a stick. It was just a pair of someone's undergarments. They told me to try it again. I said "Yes sir", knowing that I had hit the target, but I tried again. They called me "Kentucky boy". Again, they held up the target. I shot. I hit the bullseye. They played the same trick again. Up went the drawers on the stick. They told me that I would have to learn how to shoot. I knew darn well I had hit that target, not once but twice. I told them to check again! They said "You're right, you did hit it." That was some of the stuff I had to deal with at basic training. People messing with me.

I took an extra year to complete my training in the service. 3 years instead of 2. I wanted to get into the ASA. (Army Security Agency) to study Morse. I understood that if I was trained with the ASA I wouldn't necessarily need to go to combat. I would have to receive the messages and relay them from the front line to the back line. Back then they didn't have all these fancy phones like they do now adays. No texting and all that.

They sent me to Massachusetts after boot camp to learn Morse Code. It was pretty easy for me. I put the headphones on and typed what I heard. You had to pass with a certain speed. I didn't like that. I would turn the speed down so that I could type it the way I wanted to type it. One day I got called attention to the big man's office. He cut me down and said that I looked like I belonged in the boy scouts instead of the Army. This was true; I looked about 14 instead of 17. He told me that I needed to act like a man if I was going to work along side men! He wasn't pleasant. He told me to go back down and pass the test using the correct speed. I didn't really want to go to Korea or overseas. I just was a country boy from Kentucky and wanted to drive a truck or something like that. I went down and I did end up passing the test because I knew that I was a man. I was man enough not to punch the big guy in the face when he talked to me the way he did. I was again called attention to the big man's office. This time he told me to relax and that we'd talk man to man. He knew that I didn't really want to do what they were asking me to do. I told him that I just wanted to drive a truck! He questioned me, but called down to the motor pool. He told them that they had them a good man that wanted to drive himself a truck. He told me to go drive a truck and to drive it good. I said "Yes sir". That was that.

I went to Arlington Virginia. There were 12 to 15 of us. I could drive a bus. We had to drive through these cones and not hit them with the bus. I could do it! I was a pretty good driver! I had to drive the top brass of the pentagon around to where they needed to go. I was 18. I was just a country boy. I honestly had no clue what a gay guy was. I was what you called "gay bate". I looked like I was 15. In Norfolk the gay sailors took to me like glue. I learned how to avoid them. How to get rid of them. I didn't have to stay in the barracks with them anymore. I didn't want to get anyone in trouble but I didn't want to deal with all that. The government paid for me to stay in a hotel instead. It was a pretty good deal.

Another time I was with a few guys at a party in DC. There were about 30 people there. We were just hanging around having a few drinks, listening to some music, carrying on and such. In walked 3 Marines. They were trying to start something with us Army guys. There was a red-haired fellow that most people didn't mess with much. Well, all of a sudden him and another guy got into it. He took this one fella and hit him and knocked him so hard up against the wall. Someone turned off the lights and it was dark. We ended up leaving. I asked one of my buddies why we left, that he had been holding his own in there. He turned to me and said "When I hit someone 3 or 4 times as hard as I can, and they just keep coming back for more, that's when you know it's time to leave." That's why we left! I'll never forget that!

We were in a bar one night. There was a ramp that you had to walk up. Bar stools that people could sit in and then there were tables in the back where you could sit and eat if you wanted. There were people dancing and having a good time. There were these 4 Marines at this one table. Big guys. This one Marine fell on the floor and everyone laughed. It was funny. Well, I was laughing a little too loud I guess, because he came over to me and asked what I was laughing at. He told me to get up and go outside and see if I was still laughing then. I didn't say anything. He sat down. Every now and then he would come over to me and tell me that I had to leave at some point. That there was only one way out of there.

There was another guy with a sailor hat on, and he said "Go outside with that guy, and we'll see that it's fair". Turns out there were several other sailors that would go out there too. Well finally it came time for me to leave, so I said "After you, big guy", talking to the Marine. He said "Nope, after you little fella". I only weighed about 155 pounds at the time. I don't know how much the Marine weighed but he was a big guy, over 200 pounds at least. I was walking down the ramp and all of a sudden, he put his foot in my back and pushed me across the sidewalk. I fell into a parked car. He hit me 4 times. I hit him back a couple of times. I had a military ring on, with an eagle on it. I cut his cheek. He started bleeding. He was worried about the blood on his face. I jumped on his back. I was riding him piggyback. Well of course about that time these police showed up. Military police and local DC police. A couple air force guys grabbed me and we ran down this alley. They said "We'll get you out of here". I was able to get back to the base. I never looked for trouble but I never ran from trouble either. I don't claim to be a he-man.

Back at the base. I had a 1955 Ford. This was about 1958, I guess. I had been drinking a little too much to be driving. I had another guy on base with me that didn't drink, so he'd drive for me if I had been drinking too much. He was a good driver. It was a good set up because I could party and he'd drive for me. His name was "Harris".

One night I was at a party with this girl. It was a going away party for a few of the guys. I was getting bored and was ready to leave. The girl was with me, but once I left, she came too. As we were driving, she kept whining that she wanted to get back to the party. She wasn't ready to leave yet. She made me so upset, and I wanted to get her back to that party. So, I told her I would, but I was mad and driving too fast. She annoyed the heck out of me. I floored that thing going back to that party. I was driving fast. Running lights. I got pulled over. The officer checked her ID to be sure she was of age. She was. It was 3:00 in the morning. I told him the story that I was just getting her back to the party but she annoyed me.

He believed me but he couldn't just let me go. He didn't charge me for speeding. He charged me for running one red light. I thanked him. I got the girl back to the party and I went on back to the base.

One day "Harris" wanted to go home to Nelson County, Virginia. He asked if I would ride with him back home. I was 18. He introduced to me his kin folk up there. His mom and dad. Couple sisters. One of his sisters had black hair. I thought she was as pretty as a picture. She was only 14. We'd sit and play Rook at night time. Her name was Katie. She's the love of my love. I know the Lord had to have sent her to me. I don't think I could have made it with anyone but Katie. She was a little too young for me at the time, but I enjoyed her company. We'd go down there pretty often. She was the baby of 14 kids. I will say more about Katie later on.

Back on the base, not too far from there, was Harland County Kentucky. I'd take some of the guys down there. There were all kind of mountain girls. Real Daisey Mae's. We'd go down to this place called "Little Creek". We were going down there one time. There was about 3 or 4 of us in the car. I was driving pretty fast. They would run radar down there and clock you as you went by. I went around the bend. I hit the brake. I went too fast through the radar. I got a ticket. The magistrate told me I was going pretty fast. That I needed to slow down. The fine was 36 dollars. I didn't have the money. Between the 3 or 4 of us we did scrape up the money to pay the fine. He told me to slow down and take it easy. He said that he might have saved my life.

We used to go down there pretty often. The guys and I. We would drink moonshine. I would hide the moonshine in my car. I thought I was real smart. I'd drink it and sell it back at camp. One time I lost the muffler on my car. I was driving through town when I saw a state trooper. He followed me and then pulled me over. He told me that I needed a muffler on that car. I told him it was in the back of my trunk. He waited for me to get it and put it back on. When I was in the truck of my car, I saw the moonshine and I was scared to death. I thought I'd get into all kinds of trouble. I quickly put rags back over the moonshine and started to fix my car. The trooper told me to not be so nervous, to fix my car and he'd let me go. I was so happy to get that muffler back on my car and get out of there. I didn't get into trouble that night.

Another time it was late at night I was going through Gate City. There was a trooper that always set by the movie theater. I went by him and his lights went on. I didn't think I was doing anything that needed to be stopped for, so I just kept on going. I went in and out of little back roads and he didn't follow me over the line to Kentucky. I was flying. He didn't feel like messing with me anymore, I guess. Those are just a few of the stories I could tell you about my time in the army.

April the 21$^{st}$ 1960 I got out of the service. I was 20. Katie was 16 by this time. I went down to Nelson Co, Va. I stayed with that family and went to work at Morton Frozen Foods. Katie and I would go to dances together. One day I was driving Katie home from DC. Katie had graduated. She was working as a secretary in one of the federal buildings. I was taking her home. My car got stuck. My tire was just spinning. First time I ever met Katie's brother was when he picked my car up and got me unstuck. I knew then, that this was a "hoss of a man". I didn't want to mess with him. The most important part of this time of my life was the Harris family. They were good people. They were all just good people. It's because of the Army I met "Harris", which led me to Katie.

Thank you, Lord, for getting me through this part of my life.

# CHAPTER 3

# Find a job

I USED TO COOK AT A RESTAURANT ON ROUTE 250 FOR EXTRA MONEY. I always had plenty of it. At the time anyway. I enjoyed making it. The guy I worked for, was not a nice man. He was a piece of work. He had a beautiful wife and 2 girls. He would go over to West Virginia and get 2 or 3 of those mountain girls to wait the tables. I'd do the cooking. They seated a lot of people at the bar but they also had tables. They would pack the people in there. Everything was done by "hollering". They would yell out their orders. They would write up tickets, but most everyone would just holler out their orders. I got paid 100 dollars a week back then! I would work from 6 PM until 6 AM. I worked 6 days a week. We were open 24 hours.

One day my boss's wife came in wearing sun glasses. When she took them off, she had a black eye where he had beat her. I despised him! He came in a week after that and told me that he would give me an extra 20 bucks a week if I started working an extra day. So, 7 days instead of 6. I told him "I can't do that." I was already working 72 hours a week. He told me if I wanted to keep my job that I'd need to work 7 days. I took off my apron and threw it in his arms and quit. I didn't really like that job much to begin with. It's probably the only job I walked off of in my life. I didn't stay long at any job though, as I got over them pretty quickly. I was staying in Nelson County, Virginia with Katie's family. She was about 16 at the time and still in school.

When I was about 20, I went back home to where mom was. Back in Boone County Kentucky. I rented a cabin not too far from her house. She had remarried by this time. A nice guy that treated her well. He had a nice home. He was older than her but treated her nice.

In Kentucky I started a seasonal job working on the train yard. It was only a 3-month job. The pay was decent. Since I had restaurant experience, I decided to apply to another job as well. A burger place, called White Castle. They trained me. I was pretty happy with this gig. I was training for the manager position. We wore short sleeved shirts, white with a collar. I had a tattoo on my arm and you could see it with the white shirt on. Boss man told me that he didn't like that. They didn't allow tattoos to be showing. He said he could send me to a place and have it removed. I got that tattoo when I was 17. I wasn't going to do that! It's the only tattoo I have on my body! It looks alright to me. I was never ashamed of it. I wasn't going to take it off. I'm 83 years old and still have it!

There was a bus yard and I knew I was a good driver, so I thought I could drive a bus. I had to pass 6 different tests. I failed the personally test and the mechanical test. I always thought I had a good personally.

They told me to come back in 6 months and to take the tests again. I said no thanks. I thought that they must have turned away lots of good men because of their tests. I wasn't about to go through all that again. Ha!

I then went to work for an electrician. A good nice Christian man. There was this one job on a new build. I was working on the light switches. There was a little boy under 2 and a girl that was about 5. The little boy was a handful. A few days after my time with this family, I found out that the little boy got out of the house and crawled next door and a concrete truck backed over him. It was so upsetting. It hurt me really bad. Lord knows it hurt the family really bad too. After that, I couldn't quite get back into that job. I decided to move out to California.

I had a pet rabbit at the time. The rabbit would sit on my dash and ride with me. I drove my Ford out to California. Back then gas was only 27 cents a gallon. I was always picking up hitch hikers. I didn't have a lot of money with me at the time but I knew I had enough to get to California. I had 2 hitch hiker guys with me.

We were on the turnpike. I was tired and wanted a nap. I let one of the guys drive as I slept. I woke up in TX where the guy had to get out. I said, "Good enough". I went onto California. My sister was out there. I stayed there for a bit. I got a job working as a line sprayer. I had to follow this tractor and spray the weeds on the orange groves. I didn't take to that for very long.

Speaking of rabbit, I'm going to take you down a quick rabbit trail for a second. The long story short is that there was this long straight stretch in California before you got to the city limits. I knew this one guy who wanted to race me in my car. I was young. He was older. Everyone knew about him. I ended up racing him really fast in my car and ended up getting pulled over. Turns out the guy that wanted to race me, was a cop at one time. I ended up getting let go because I told them the story about this guy and how he kept wanting to race me in my car. The other guy wasn't a good influence to a young kid like me. I never knew what happened to him, but they were not really happy with him trying to influence me in this way. The cop let me go and told me to drive safe.

I got tired of California and decided to go back home. I picked up a hitch hiker in TX. We went to Mexico for a few days and had a good time. We stopped at a liquor store and I bought some bourbon. I hid some under some cardboard in the back. I had 3 bottles of liquor in the front with us. Well, when we went to get by the guard, he asked me if I had anything to claim. I told him that we had 3 bottles of unopened liquor. Well, we were only allowed to have one each. I knew this. The guard told me to give him one. He let me go on my merry way. The hitch hiker said "That was a pretty good trick". That whiskey was so smooth.

I've done a lot of dumb things in my life. I guess it was just another dumb thing I got away with.

I used to drive a dump truck and sell some coal too. It was a 1939 Dodge. I'd play poker. I'd play "TONK". This was in Kentucky. There was a lot of mountain people. They were rough and tough. The houses were just shacks. There were rats. You could see between the slits in the floor. When it snowed, you would get a little snow on your blanket. I drank a lot during this time in my life. Anyone would take me in. I could stay wherever I wanted. I had a girl in my life then. She was a pretty girl. A stockier girl but pretty. Long story short, she got around. I was cocky as ever. I drank too much. She jumped on me and punched me. Gave me a black eye. My eye was swollen shut. Word got around. I looked like I was beat up and everyone knew she had done it. It took a few days for this to clear up. A few weeks later her grandfather saved me from a guy. The long story short of this, is that her grandfather saved me from something there. I needed to get out of that mess. I was thankful.

Back in Kentucky, I had a rock crusher and I had a job to build a road. It was ½ a mile road. There was an old shack on it. I wanted to buy these 18 acres from the guy who owed it. I wanted to buy it for 1200 dollars. It was in the "Walton" area. This was in 1961. I got 18 acres and a shack for 1200 dollars.

Well, I had a girlfriend that was "something else". I had a good time with her. She could dance. We could dance "jitter bug". She liked too many guys though. She got around. She went with anybody and everybody. She became pregnant. She told me I was a daddy. I had a hard time believing her story. I had no reason to know that was mine. I knew I needed to get out of that mess. She told me it was mine but there was no way to know. I sold my dump truck. My horse. The 18 acres. The property was sold for 3900 dollars. I needed to get out of there and get back to Virginia. I bought myself a car and still had 400 or 500 dollars. I went to Nelson County. I asked about Katie. She had graduated. She was working for the government. I didn't want this little girl to get by me. She was in DC. I had to get there.

In 1962 I got myself another car. It was a convertible. I had an apartment in DC. My car got stolen. I filed a report. I ended up getting arrested for being a "peeping" Tom, but that wasn't the case at all. It was 3 a.m. and I was waiting for my ride. Turns out my story was true. They let me go. They found my car. All torn up. It was considered demolished. It was such a pretty car too.

Me and Katie, we dated awhile. She was the baby of 14 kids like I said before. They didn't have electricity when she grew up. Her daddy liked to drink. So, did I. As long as I had the liquor, he liked me pretty good. Half of her family liked me. The other half questioned why Katie was even interested in a guy like me. Katie has always been good at everything she did. Except for maybe marrying me. She's stood by my side for 61 years though. (*God bless her!!*) I know that God was on my side. Katie was the love of my life. As long as her daddy went a long with it, I wanted to marry her.

Thank you, Lord, for getting me through this time in my life.

# CHAPTER 4

# Got Married

I WAS LIVING IN AN APARTMENT IN DC WITH A ROOMMATE AT THE time. I wanted to get married to Katie. I bought her an engagement ring. I'm not sure what's wrong with me, but when I gave the ring to Katie, she wasn't as excited as I thought she should be. I got upset and kicked the coffee table.

All of a sudden, I get a knock on the door. There was a guy I used to work for, and standing with him, was the girl that supposably was carrying my child. He told me that I needed to do the right thing and marry this girl. I liked her but not enough to marry her. I told him that I wasn't even sure the child was mine. I wasn't going to marry someone who I couldn't trust. She wanted anyone and everyone. She'd been with too many guys. It was out of the question. She wanted me to marry her until the baby was born and then if I didn't want her and the baby, I could divorce her. I couldn't do that. I had just asked Katie to marry me. They left. This was about 4 months before I was to marry Katie. I have made a lot of mistakes in my life. Katie should have just given me back the ring and walked away. She didn't. She decided to marry me anyway.

In 1963, on January 12th, we got married. She was 19 and I was 23. It was 3 days after my birthday, Jan 9th. We were married in Nelson County Virginia, in a little Methodist church that sat on a hill. It was a gift from God. God has been good to me. Some of her family didn't exactly oppose it, but not everyone was for it either. In a way, marrying Katie was like being born again. I had already asked God into my life, but this was a new beginning for me.

I was working in DC at a place called Drug Fair. I had to deliver drugs to places in DC and down in Virginia. They had 14 drivers. I was the only white driver. It was back in 1963. Everyone else was black. I had a guy riding with me and back then he couldn't eat in the restaurant, so I'd eat in my truck with him. I never considered myself prejudice. They started protesting back then. 1964. Martin Luther King was a good man. A God-fearing man. A peaceful, honest man. He meant well for his people. I had always gotten along well with everyone but that year I became a "cracker this and a cracker that". Things weren't the same once all the marching and the lining up in the streets happened. They didn't take to me real well anymore. The plan was to tear down the relationships between the black people and the white people. We're still dealing with this in this county now more so than ever. We're so divided as a country. I can't believe that things are still the way they are today. I'm 83 years old, so I know I won't have to live too much longer in this place, but I hate to think what my grandkids have to go through!

Working at Drug Fair, you had a lot of drugs for the pharmacy. There were several stores we went to. They had stacks of boxes. Every 6 months we had to take a polygraph test. I never worried about anything because I knew I wasn't stealing anything. There was stuff missing from some of my stuff and another guy. There was 3 of us working one day. There was a black guy that was a preacher. Turns out he'd steal a couple boxes from my truck and the other guy's truck. He was such a "good guy" that no one paid any attention to him. When he'd make his stops, he'd take what he had stolen from us and put it in the cab of his truck. They found out. They were going to fire him. Everyone wondered how he passed the polygraph. He was able to pass the polygraph because he had a pencil in his pocket. He'd tell the story that when he was questioned about taking anything that he didn't pay for, he'd pull out the pencil and say, "Well yes, I didn't pay for this and I didn't take it back after I used it". So, he was able to get away with that. He used the pencil to help with the story and the test. I don't know how he could do that!

I was so bothered by the polygraph test that there was this one time I picked out a comic book at one store in Maryland. I was looking at it and then I put it on a box in my truck and didn't think anything of it. Well after my shift, this bothered me so bad, I knew I had to take this comic book back to the store in Maryland.

I went back to the manager of the store and told him the story. I wanted to be sure I'd be able to pass that polygraph test. I didn't want a 10-cent comic book to be holding me back. The guy couldn't believe it. I put it back on the shelf. It was in good shape but I offered to pay for it if the manager wanted me to. He thought I was crazy.

On the routes, sometimes we had to wait 20 or 30 minutes for the managers to come unlock the lock boxes with the drugs inside. I used to watch people shoplift all the time. 90 percent of the time they would just let the people go. One time a man dressed in a nice suit stole good expensive cigars but only paid for a cheap one. I saw the whole thing go down and told the manager. The manager told me that I was wrong. That the man came in all the time. He knew him by name. I looked like a guy that would be doing the steeling because I was dressed in casual clothes, not in the nice suit like the other man. Turns out, I was right. The man in the suit said it was a mistake and paid for the cigars. The store manager told him to not come back again. I saw stuff like this happen all the time. Another time I saw a guy taking a tv and some shirts right off the rack. I ran after him. He threw the TV at me and kept on running. He kept the shirts and took off again. Finally, he dropped the shirts and ran. There was a cop waiting down by the alley and caught him. I could tell you all kinds of stories. I got so fed up with this job. I told Katie that I had kept it long enough to prove to her mama, but that I was done with it.

Thank you, Lord, for this time of my life.

# CHAPTER 5

# Buying a Home

I QUIT MY JOB WITH DRUG FAIR. I WENT TO WORK SELLING VACUUM cleaners. Rainbow vacuum cleaners. Door to door selling them. It cost over 300 dollars per vacuum. It was something else. That was a pile of money especially way back then. I made 70 dollars for every vacuum I sold. I could sell that vacuum cleaner! I could show the customers how their vacuum cleaned, then use mine, and show how good it did. It was a great selling point! It did a good job this vacuum. I did pretty good at that job for a while, until I saw that "Best" had a vacuum on sale for cheaper than mine. Every one of those could pick up dust or dirt! They cost less. Most of the people I was selling the vacuum to couldn't afford it anyway. They would take the vacuum on a payment plan. That bothered me terribly. I told Katie I was going to quit that job. Katie was working for the government at this time. She had a steady full-time job.

Our first son was born 9 months and 10 days after we got married. I tell that story because that's the way it was. You know how people are. Thinking that we were pregnant before we got married. That's not how it was. So, I tell the story that he was born 9 months and 10 days after we got married. Not that it matters what people think, but anyway. I didn't want people thinking that.

We bought a house in Morningside, Maryland. I quit the vacuum job and went to work for Sterling Laundry. That was a job and a half. Most people paid their bill on time but every so often I had to knock on doors and try to collect the payment. Most people would just leave their laundry in bags outside the door. I'd grab the laundry and leave. Well, there was this one stop. There was this one girl. White girl, she was married to a black guy. They had white and black everything. The sofa, the carpet, even their dogs were white and black. There was nothing wrong with that. Most of the time she wouldn't have the laundry ready. I'd have to knock on the door and I'd have to wait on her to get her stuff together. I'd hand her the stuff that was already done and clean, and she'd give me the stuff that needed to be washed. This one time she said, I haven't even taken the sheets off the bed yet, it will only take a minute. She told me to come on in. She was only wearing a little night outfit this day. Hardly anything on. You could see right through it. She asked me to come in and help her take the sheets off the bed. I wasn't going to have anything to do with all that. She soon learned that I wasn't going to do that type of thing. I came home and told Katie about it. I quit this job. In the meantime, I had told Katie that I had wanted to move back to Kentucky. Katie loved her job and had been there a few years. We'd only been married about a year.

Katie was not happy about selling our house to move. She hadn't even told her job that we were moving by the time the house sold. It sold pretty quickly to a young couple that went to the church down the street from it. I was able to make a little money off the house and that was good by me. I told Katie to tell her job we were leaving! Corven (our son) and I were going to go back to Kentucky. I said it's up to you if you'll be with us or not. I was a jerk! She finally gave a weeks' notice, at work. She was upset that day. I haven't seen her upset that many times in my life but she was upset that day. Depressed almost. She didn't want to leave or to move. We loaded up everything we had / everything we wanted. That truck was loaded down! I knew I'd have a hard time getting it over the mountains, so I put Katie and Corven on a plane and I said I'd drive all our stuff to Kentucky. I was going to meet them there!

My mom found a house we could rent. We were on our way to Kentucky! A few things fell off the truck as I went over the mountains, but I just kept right on going. If it fell off, then we didn't need it anyway. We were in Kentucky!

Thank you, Lord, for getting us though this time in our lives.

# CHAPTER 6

# Made Dad a Partner

WHILE WE WERE IN KENTUCKY, I HAD A COUPLE THOUSAND DOLLARS from the sale of the house in Maryland, so I rented a little corner grocery store and stocked it with a few things. It was the low-income side of Covington. I rented it. Started stocking it. Quart beer, deli meat, hot dogs, sodas, different groceries, etc. Lots of the soda places would help me get started by giving me one case of soda, and I'd buy the others. Pepsi was a buy one get one type of deal. Root Bear did the same thing. 7UP. RC Cola. Everyone did this except for Coke. Coke wouldn't give me a deal. So, I said, "Fine, I'll put a sign on my door saying "No Coke sold here!". The guy laughed at me and said that I couldn't open a store without Coke! He said I was a foolish man! I told him I'd prove him wrong. That I could open up a store without Coke. If I was foolish, then so be it! I wasn't going to do business with Coke unless they gave me a deal like everyone else. I was doing pretty good. Lots of traffic. Just a corner store. Soap, breads, little grocery type items. When people came in, they would ask me about the sign on the door. Coke didn't like this! I told the people the truth! Coke wouldn't give me a deal so I didn't want to sell their product here. Coke decided they wanted to make this situation right. They said they don't normally make deals but that they would with me. I told them to give me 20 cases of Coke and I'd buy 10 of them. They agreed to do this. This little corner store got to be a little too much for me to handle on my own. I decided to make my dad a partner! Yes, the same dad that beat the crap out of me as a child. My dad was a meat butcher by trade. I knew that he could help me run the deli side of things. I told him that he could have half of everything we made. We were partners. Dad would work the back. I'd work front and back. Dad's girlfriend ran the register. Well, it got to the point where it went to Dad's head. He'd just come and take 20 or 30 bucks out of the register any time he wanted. It got to the point that I told my dad I wasn't going to keep doing business with him anymore. We got in an argument over this. Vivian, my dad's girlfriend called the cops. My dad was a likeable guy. Everyone knew him. He was respected by everyone but family. He treated family terrible.

We didn't have a contract written up or anything official. Dad and I were partners. He had half of the store and I had the other half. I gave dad the store. I told dad he needed to give me 1500 and the store was his. He told me to get out. That was that. I went to work for a drive-in restaurant at this time.

Dad never did send me any money for the store. I went to talk with him about this one day. We got into it. Dad wasn't going to pay me. Dad grabbed me by my shirt collar and ripped my suit. Pushed me. Dad grabbed a Pepsi bottle and broke it. "Hell" flew into me. I hit him a few times. We kept on. We went through the whole store. Knocking stuff all over the place. Dad hit his cheek on a nail and cut it open. He started to bleed. I felt sorry for him. Vivian called the police. They came. They grabbed me and said to my dad, "What do you want us to do with him Matthew?" Dad said, "Nothing, but I don't want him coming back here again". I left. So basically, Dad got the goldmine, I got the shaft. And that was that.

In Kentucky, Katie went to work for a country music station. Everyone loved Katie. She could get a good job anywhere. She was asked to go and represent the station when Webb Pierce (a great music entertainer) was coming to do a concert in the area. She was given a back room pass to personally meet him. When he saw Katie, He leaned over to hug her and gave her a little kiss on the cheek. I didn't like that. I was jealous even though I didn't need to be. Katie was mine and no one else's. I acted like that. I treated her that way. I was that way. I didn't like any other man hugging on Katie. Not long after that, I told Katie we were moving to California. We were not in Kentucky long. Once again Katie was forced to quit and leave a job she loved.

Thank you, God, for getting us through this time in our lives.

# CHAPTER 7

## Move to California

WE MOVED OUT TO CALIFORNIA. ON THE WAY THERE IN THE DEAD boring desert, I remember thinking "Man, God must have gotten tired in this place, because there wasn't anything pretty at all. It was nothing to look at! It was so hot there! Rocky mountain. Useless country".

Anyway, in California we got a nice little house. Nice yard. It was beautiful. Rose bushes and everything. Sprinkler system. We had a refrigerator that the door didn't close correctly. I had to rig up something to keep it shut. Once my brother-in-law said to me, "When are you going to buy that woman something?" He said "Get her nice refrigerator". I said I wasn't going to go into debt over a refrigerator. That's just the way I was.

Katie was looking for a job. She went to Aerospace Corporation to fill out an application. Once she was done, the manager came out and saw that she had filled out the application. He asked if she could really type and take shorthand as fast as she put on her application. He told her that they were not hiring, but to come take the shorthand test and the typing test. She passed with flying colors. He told her to give him a week and they would make an opening for her! They hired her! Everyone loved Katie.

I went to work for 2 Jews. Selling new and used furniture. I was good at selling. I'm working at this furniture store. These Military guys would come in looking for furniture. One time this guy ordered a whole house full of stuff! It was a really good sale! We were unloading all the stuff he ordered. There was one night table that hand a scratch on it and the guy said "That's not going to work. Take that back". There was another piece of furniture that also had a scratch on it where it had rubbed against something. He didn't want that piece either. We took both pieces back to the store. I told him we'd replace them both. Every piece in the store had the same mark on them. It must have been a manufacturing issue. I took some shoe polish and I buffed out the scratches really good. They looked 100 times better than they did before I had done that! If you looked really close, you could still see the scratches, but I figured we'd try it. I thought the guy might have an issue with it, but we went on anyway. We got them into the house and I told the guy it was the best I could do. He paid me and that was that. This went on for a while.

This one time this black lady came in and saw a picture hanging on the wall in the store. She asked how much it was. I knew she didn't have much. Boss man said it was 13 dollars. She wanted to give us 3 dollars then and pay the rest off, before Christmas. Back then, they had these other stores that carried the exact same picture for 9 dollars and 99 cents! This bothered me so much!! I told the boss man this. I wasn't happy. I ended up quitting that job and going to a place called, Brookside Dairy. They did home deliveries. Some of these stops were 3:00 in the morning. We'd stop at these Indian reservations. The government paid their bill for them. They just wanted anything they could get!

There were a few stops that you'd have to bring in cold milk that was in glass bottles. This one place had a nice home. They had several adopted kids. This place had a swimming pool. There was a girl about 2 years old.

I was worried about that baby getting out and getting into that pool. The lady said I had nothing to worry about. That they always taught the kids how to swim as soon as they came to live there. It wasn't a week later that that baby drowned in that pool. After that, the delivery to that house had been cut off. She didn't want to face me again and I didn't want to face her again either. It was fine by me. That poor little baby! I ended up quitting the dairy job and I went to work for JC Penney in the men's department. I had wanted to get a job in the restaurant industry but out there, no one would hire me because I didn't have a degree to back me up. I'll get back to this story in a bit.

During this time in California, our second son Breck was born. He was 4 years younger than Corven. I remember praying to God to keep Katie and the baby safe. Breck wasn't going to wait for the doctor. He was born in the prep room at the hospital. He was safe and so was Katie. I had prayed to God a lot during this time. I was suffering a lot with back pain. I ended up going to the doctor and getting injections in my spine. I felt like a weight was lifted off me after that. I really feel like God was keeping Katie and Breck safe, and I was the one suffering with the back pain. So now we had 2 kids.

As I was working at JC Penney, I'd often go into this café across the street on my lunch break. It was called Oscar's Café. They had bar stools and two tables. They were busy all the time. The lady who owned the place, was named Tilly. They had Mexican food and it was good. I couldn't believe how good it was. Tilly was Mexican. There was another girl working there who couldn't speak any English. The place was so busy, there would be people sitting in the stools and then they would have a line waiting. It was always this way. As I said before, I had wanted to be in the restaurant industry but no one would hire me because I didn't have a high school education or the manager experience. At this point we had the 2 kids and 4 mouths to feed. One day Tilly asked if I was interested in helping with the restaurant. She was going to go back to Mexico for a year. I was to help Isabelle in the café and help run the place until she got back. Isabelle couldn't speak any English and I couldn't speak any Spanish, but we made do. I watched and I learned. During this year I watched the way Isabelle did everything. I got to be really good at it. Everything she fixed, I learned how. I would write it down. Enchiladas, tacos, beans, you name it. Well, we did this for a year. Once Tilly came back, I'm not exactly sure what happened, but she wasn't real happy with the way the place was being run. I had done everything she asked me to do, but I knew it was time to for me to leave. I told Katie, yet again, it was time for her to quit her job. We were going to move back to Kentucky.

Katie wasn't happy. She had been at Aerospace for a couple of years. We had 2 kids, one 4 and one just a baby. It was time for us to leave though.

Thank you, God, for this time in our lives.

# CHAPTER 8

# Move back to Kentucky

We sold almost everything but kept a few things to start up the house at a new place. We had lots of heavy jars of beans and stuff we were taking with us. The car was loaded down. I had a cousin at the time that wanted to come back to Kentucky too. We were going to follow each other. He had his family in his car and I had my family in mine. We set off for Kentucky. For some reason my cousin had the baby's milk in his car. Not too far from the California line, our car broke down. I figured my cousin would come back for us. He never did. He was a piece of work.

We sat on the side of the road for so long and someone finally came along and asked if we needed some help. They pulled us in a Wrecker into Needles, and we got a Motel there. Got milk for the baby. They told us that we needed a new motor put in. They told me it was going to cost most of the money that we had. But we needed it! They told me that the car was too loaded down. Some of the stuff would have to go. I had to get rid of the canned beans and jars of stuff we had. I donated it to a local shelter there. We put in the new motor. We had a little money left over for gas and food until we got back to Kentucky.

We managed to make it to Kentucky. Saw my cousin. He said "I didn't know what happened to you". I said, "You could have come back to check on us!" I was upset but at that point we just had to move on. I had to take things where they were, what's done was done.

Our plan was to stay in Kentucky, but after about a month and a half, our plans changed once more. Turns out we would be moving yet again, and this time to Virginia. Funny the plans we have for our lives, and yet the Lord directs our paths.

I ended up getting a job in Virginia. Thank you, God, for this time in our lives.

# CHAPTER 9

# Kenny Burger

We left Kentucky and headed to Virginia. We rented a little house behind the fire house. I went to work driving a school bus and working in a country grocery store. Katie went to work for Acme, a factory in Crozet. As I was working in the store and driving a bus, I met a guy named "Wood". He worked in one of the Kenny Burger stores. There were 3 stores at the time. They were looking for a manager in one of the stores. They wanted to hire me. They said that I would need to work for 6 days a week. There was a bonus involved but it wasn't enough money for what I wanted. I told them I would work 7 days a week until I proved to them that I could run the store.

They said they would give me 125 dollars a week. I told them, nope. Not enough. I told them 150 dollars a week! I wasn't going to come for less than that!! I had 2 kids and 4 mouths to feed. I said you pay me 150 dollars a week for 2 weeks, and if I'm not worth everything I said I would be, keep it and let me go!

Finally, they agreed. There was only one other manager at that time making that kind of money. They sent me to Waynesboro for training.

Then to Harrisonburg for a few more days of training. Then I was to go to the store in Charlottesville.

The other manager was fired. He wasn't doing a good job. There it was. I had the Charlottesville store.

I had a crew of 14 people. High school kids. They were wild. This one kid would get himself a hot dog when he wasn't working and didn't pay for it. I didn't like this. I told the kid I wasn't the old manager, and I don't do things the way he did. This kid didn't like that much. I wanted to let him go and hire someone else.

At this point I asked Katie to come work for me. We were really busy. She ran the register. We were the number one fast food place in that area. By the end of the year, I brought that place out of the hole and made them 4 thousand dollars. I was making my monthly bonus every month too. I was pretty proud of myself.

There was this one supervisor that had 2 families. One in Charlottesville and one in Waynesboro. He was a piece of work! His wife in Waynesboro didn't know about the other family. He had kids with 2 different women. One night, his second wife called me and needed him to come there right away. He made up a story to his wife, that the restaurant had been broken into. He threw a rock at the window and told me to call the police. This was the type of man he was. He was always doing fishy things. Always in some type of situation. I wouldn't let him get away with anything in my store! There was a hobo guy that he would give money out of the petty cash drawer for cleaning windows. I told him that wasn't going to happen at my store! We cleaned our own windows. He did dirty business.

We lived in Nelson County at the time. I'd stop at these little county stores sometimes on my way home. They had pool tables in a few of these places. I was playing pool. In walked this rough individual. He looked like death! He was trying to pick a fight with this one guy, so I knew that I needed to get out of there. I left and went down to the next store on the way home. I was playing pool again. The same rough individual came in to that store too. He had 2 other guys with him. He challenged me to a game of pool. He wanted to play. He grabbed my arm and asked to play a game. He wanted to play for a dollar. He wasn't a good shot. I lost that game and I let him win. I wanted to go on home. He grabbed my arm again and said we'd play again and this time for 2 dollars. I won that game. This other guy said "Dave you won that game, he owes you 2 dollars". When I asked the guy for the money, he hit me in the face and knocked me across the pool table. He made me feel so small, I ended up going to my car and getting my pistol. It was just a 22, I think. I pointed it to his nose and said "Give me my 2 dollars". He told me that I was going to have to shoot him. I hit him up beside his head with the pistol. He didn't flinch. He kept coming. I shot the floor. He kept coming. I got out in the parking lot. Shot again. He kept coming. I had 2 shots left. I shot him in the foot. He went down on one knee. I knew I had 1 shot left but they thought that was it. I got in my car. I rolled down my window and said I had another shot left and that if anyone else laid a hand on me, I'd shoot them between the eyes. I told Katie about all this. She said "What were you thinking!". I called the police. They already had a report and said that a deputy was on the way over to get me. I was told that the guy that fought with me had just gotten out of prison the week before. That he was "death on wheels". The deputy said that he would need to take me that night! I talked him into letting me go in the morning instead. I needed someone to bail me out. I sure picked a bad guy to deal with. I thought I was going to get 3 to 5 years in jail. The boy was something else. He was limping because he had a bullet in his foot. I told my side of the story. He agreed to it. He had broken his parole. He didn't want to go back to prison. It was decided that for one year, we both had to behave ourselves, and stay out of trouble. After the year was up, if we kept our word, this whole thing would be dropped off the books. I was so relieved! I left there. I went back to Charlottesville. Went back to work. Told the supervisor. He said I was lucky. I said, "That is what prayer does for you."

I was scared that this guy would come back and hurt my family. I wanted us to get away from that little country store where I had gotten in that trouble. We stayed in Stuarts Draft with family until I could find us a place.

We found a duplex not far from the restaurant. Katie and I worked together. We worked well together. I hired back the kid that I had let go before, because he impressed me and kept on coming back. There was another kid too. He might have done some drugs but he was a really good employee. I went through about 85 employees before I ended up with a good crew. I had 3 good guys helping me run the line. I say this, because I am pretty proud of these boys. One of the boys went on to DJ in NY. Another one ended up as a supervisor for Kroger's. The other kid graduated and went into the Air Force. He retired as a 4-star general and was with the Air Force for 25 years or so. I'm proud that these guys worked for me. One of these guys had a girlfriend named Shelly. She worked for me too. They ended up getting married. Whenever they were in Charlottesville, they would come see me. He thanked me for helping him to become the man he is today. He helped me a lot and I told him that he became the man he is today, because he chose to become that way. I've always been proud of him!

After a year of working with Kenny Burgers, I was ready to leave if I didn't get a raise. I asked for 25 dollars more a week. So, 175 dollars a week. I told them that I wanted that or I was going to leave. In the meantime, I was looking for a place that I could buy to open up a restaurant of my own. My mom was in Kentucky, and by this time, her second husband had died. She had broken up with her third husband and had agreed to come help me in Charlottesville at this restaurant. I borrowed 1500 dollars. She would put up 1500 dollars and we'd get ourselves a place. She agreed to that. Meanwhile, the vice president of Kenny Burger decided that I was worth a raise. They wanted to give me my own car, and make me the supervisor of 4 stores. I appreciated that, but I told them I was leaving to go open up my own place. They weren't exactly happy about this. They tried to find anything they could find against me, but there was nothing to find. They wished me luck and I left.

Thank you, God, for this time in our lives.

# CHAPTER 10

# La Hacienda

I ENDED UP FINDING A PLACE FOR THE RESTAURANT I WAS INTERESTED in starting. The guy who owned it was named Jerry Moore. I'll never forget him. He gave me my opportunity. I told him what I wanted to do. Jerry wanted me to serve American food, as well as Mexican. I had to be open 7 days a week. And open for breakfast too. I could close on Christmas only. He wanted to give me a year lease. He agreed to this, but told me I had to give him 10 thousand dollars for the equipment that was in this place if I wanted to stay another year. He didn't want to mess with it! Everything was "alright" by me. I rented it! I got in contact with Pepsi. They put a machine in there and some syrup to help get me started. The Dairy gave me a freezer, some milk and ice cream, stuff to get me started. I had enough space in the freezer so I also kept fries in there.

We opened up on June the 6$^{th}$ 1970. We were the first Mexican restaurant in Charlottesville. Not only were we the first Mexican restaurant in Charlottesville, but also in Virginia. I knew that people were coming from all over the country to go to school in Charlottesville. It's a college town. I knew that if the Mexican place did as well as it did in California, that we could do that in Virginia too. This was 50 years ago. Corven was working in the back washing dishes. He was 7 years old. He'd rinse and then put them in the dishwasher. Mom was working out front with Katie and a couple other girls. Another guy was helping me cook. We were so busy. I had to lock the front door just so that we could serve the people in the place. We had to get them fed before we had room for anyone else. We had opened up a goldmine.

The menu we used for 26 years, the cover, was drawn up by a kid that helped wash dishes in the back.

When I quit Kenny Burger, one of the guys, the one that went on to be the Air Force General, came to help me at this place when he had time after school.

I think now would be a good time for me to tell you a story about what this whole thing is about. Partners. We're born into the partnership with the government. We choose the partnership with the Lord. If it hadn't had been for the Lord, I don't know how I would have gotten through some of this stuff. The government, you cannot do anything without him having his nose in everything you do. When I was in the food business, I had to pay 17 different taxes. Food tax, sales tax, meals tax, liquor tax, business tax, gas tax. I could go on and on. There was 17 of them! Every one of them had to be paid by the customers. That's the only way I could pay the tax! The government made more money off of every meal that I sold than I could have even thought of making!

Anyway, this restaurant was busy. We were doing pretty well. It was a dynamite business. Mom was a partner in this. As I said before, we opened it with 3 thousand dollars. She owned hers, I had to borrow mine, but it was jointly owned by us both.

I hired this guy named Charles from a farm in Gordonsville. He was the best employee. He worked for me for 26 years. He was as "clean as a whistle". He and mom worked well together. He was the head cook.

During the first year that we were opened, I had a couple come into the restaurant. I served the black and brown bean combo that I learned how to make from Isabelle back in California. The couple liked their meal. They wanted to meet the manager who cooked. I introduced myself. The couple said that they wanted to "help" me. They said that my beans looked nasty. They tried to tell me what I should do instead. They told me to get rid of my beans! I never changed that menu for the 26 years that I was in business. The only thing I ever changed on that menu was the prices. The rest of the menu stayed the same.

I had been in there a year or two when the local paper wanted to interview me. I was the only Mexican restaurant at the time. They asked me if there was anyone who had "helped" me along the way. Of course, I had people help me. Can't get anywhere in life without help. This newspaper interview reminded me of the couple that came in that day to "help" me. I told them that they complained about the beans. The couple was from NY. They wanted me to get my beans off the menu if I wanted to be successful. The moral of the story, is that I ended up not taking their advice but keeping what I had learned in CA and I've done well for myself. In fact, I was getting ready to open up another restaurant up in Staunton.

Two years after we opened our first restaurant, our daughter Cyndra was born. We now had three children. The two boys and a baby girl. Business kept rolling on, and we kept expanding as things fell into place.

Thank you, God, for this time in our lives.

# CHAPTER 11

# El Cabrito's

The second year we were in business we opened the Staunton location. I found a free-standing building. I owned this one outright. Mom wasn't a partner in this location. She kept an eye on the Charlottesville one. I opened a third La Hacienda in Harrisonburg. By this time, we had the one in Charlottesville doing amazing, and the one in Staunton was doing pretty well. So, we found a place in Harrisonburg for the third location. This was in the third year or so. Everywhere I went, the government kept their nose in everything. If you didn't know how to handle them, they could drive you nuts.

This location was a dirty place. We cleaned it up really good. It needed a lot of work but it looked 100 times better than when I found it. It has been a restaurant before I took it over. It took us weeks to get that place cleaned up. I needed a health permit and a business license. The health department said I needed a paper towel rack before I could open. I did it. The guy was arrogant. He said he'd keep an eye on me. He was going to be sure that I was keeping this place clean. There's no way that place could have been any dirtier than how it was when I first took it over. Our tax dollar goes to pay for these guys salaries. It's unbelievable.

There was this one time I had a cook in there working. It was a busy time, right during lunch. This guy from the health department came in and was following my cook around. Jerry the cook, was trying to work but the health department man was trying to do his job too, just not at a very good time. There were customers waiting, people eating, food cooking, he could have come back at a less busy time. That's not how it went down. My cook Jerry didn't appreciate this guy very much and he let him know it! He chased the health department worker out of the door with a skillet. The girl I had managing this location called me right then and I said I'd be there as soon as I could. Jerry told me his side of the story.

I went to the health department to talk to whoever was in charge. They said they were going to try to close up this location. I had to talk with Jerry and told him he'd need to settle down. I also had to tell the health inspector that he needed to not just come in there and tell Jerry what he needed to do.

It was my restaurant. Not Jerry's. Not the health inspectors! We were able to settle everyone down. They let me keep on operating this place. What a headache!

This was about the same time I decided to open a small office to keep all the books straight. Shelly and Katie ran this place. They paid all the bills, did payroll, etc. Then I wanted to open up a hot dog and chili place in Staunton. A little stand of some sort. That's what I did. I had a lot of help! I had about 150 employees at one point between all my places.

Well, I got it in my head, that I wanted to open up a fast-food restaurant. Kind of like a Taco Bell. It would have a limited menu. Tacos, burritos, etc.

I got myself a builder to do what I wanted across from Albemarle High

School, in Charlottesville. Mr. Harris was his name. He made this building look like stucco on the outside. We called this place El Cabrito's. It opened and did well. We also opened a second location with the same name, same type of building. This one was up in Fredericksburg.

Then I had another guy who wanted to do business with me. A third location in Lynchburg with this same name. I told him if he could get someone to build a building like these other two locations, I'd do it! That's what we did! I now had three locations with El Cabrito's name. Business was doing well!

Thank you, God, for this time in our lives.

# CHAPTER 12

# Nine Restaurants

By this point, we had the three La Hacienda locations, three El Cabrito's locations, and the two chili dog shops.

On the way to the third El Cabrito's location, in Lynchburg, there was a town called Amherst. I had to pass right through there. There was a little restaurant in a shopping center there. A family style place. Free standing. Nice place! The guys who owned it, wanted to make a deal with me. They said that the rent for the first year would be cheaper, but then after that, they expected to get more. They asked me to take it over. I liked the idea. I was going through that area anyway. I opened that place and called it Pappy's Mountain Fried Chicken. We cooked this chicken in a pressure cooker type thing. I found a lady to run this place and manage it. We were doing pretty well there.

Katie took care of all the payroll and paid all our bills. As I said before, we had about 150 employees at this time. The government was everywhere. Every kind of inspector came in from all over the place. Every kind of tax you could think of. We were paying all the inspectors salaries by this point but they never liked when I said that to them. They never wanted to hear all that.

I had been in business about 6 or 7 years when the next big situation would happen to us.

Thank you, God, for getting us through this time in our lives.

# CHAPTER 13

# IRS

In 1977, I had a bookkeeper that had done my taxes, quarterlies and stuff; in Winchester. Now you might wonder, "Why in Winchester?" Well, I didn't want anybody from Charlotteville, Staunton, Harrisonburg or anyone from around here doing them for me, because I didn't want them sitting around a cocktail table talking about my business. So, I got this bookkeeper from up there. That's my first mistake.

I never had an accountant. The IRS was going to come in and audit me for '74, '75, and '76. I said okay. So, I had bought a piece of property down in Amherst. Well mom bought it. It was a nice buy. I don't remember 40 or 50 acres, fenced. Pasture. I put some cattle on it. This IRS guy, agent, was gonna check me out, to see what all I was doing wrong. He was trying to see if they could get some more money out of me. He was in Staunton. I can't think of his name. I can remember some of the other's names, but I can't remember his.

So, I took him all the information that he wanted on '74, '75, and '76. They could only go back 3 years. I don't know what the rules are today, but back then they could only go back 3 years if they didn't find any fraud on you. He was doing '74 and he said, "I saw that you took a loss on a couple of cows down in Amherst. You can't do that." He said that was more of a hobby. I said, "What do you mean I can't do that? That ain't no hobby! I don't do anything for a hobby." If I lost the money, I lost the money and that's the way it's going to be. So, he asked for some other records and information. I said, okay and was very cooperative. I gave him whatever he asked for, whatever he needed.

I was supposed to take all this to his Staunton office. I laid it on his office table. He was sitting behind his desk. I told him, "You know, it looks to me like, after all, it's my tax dollars that pays your salary; it looks to me like you could be doing this for me as well as for the government, just so you get the right thing done." He glanced up at me and kind of grinned. I didn't like that. So, I said to him. "What are you grinning at? What's so funny?" He said "That's not the way it goes".

Well, that upset me. I said, "That's not the way it goes?". He said "no". I said, "We'll that's the way this audits gonna go. If you can't treat me like a human being, then this is over". I reached over and grabbed a stack of stuff that he already had sitting there that belonged to me, and the stuff I brought, and I put it all in a box. I said, "When you can treat me like a human being, you can call me back and I'll come back here and we'll sit down and see if we can't work something out." "You can't do that," he said! I said, "I am doing it", and I walked out. I took the records I had left for him for '74.

So about 30 days went by and then he called me and asked if I could meet him over in Staunton. I said sure. I thought we were gonna work something out. I go in the office. There's two guys in there with him. I'll never forget them. They took out their badges. They said they were from the Criminal Investigation of the IRS. They said, "Now you have a right to have an attorney present if you want."

I said I guess that would be a pretty good idea. So, I went over into the other office there and called my attorney, in Waynesboro. He was an attorney friend I played poker with him and a bunch of other guys. I told him on the phone what was happening. He said "Oh my gosh Dave. Tell them that we'll get with them". I said "No, wait a minute, I ain't done nothing wrong. I'm not letting these people push me around. No way in Hell!" My attorney said, "Well I know how stubborn you can be, but now this is serious". I said "I don't care. I'm mainly calling you so that if they lock me up today, you make arrangements to bail me out." He said "Alright".

So, I hung the phone up and went back to the office where they were at. They asked if I wanted to wait on my attorney. I said "No, I don't need an attorney. I haven't done anything wrong". They said, "Well if that's the case then you have nothing to worry about". I said "That's the case".

Well, I sat down there for 2 days. They took all my records for '74, '75, and '76. They put it all in station wagons and carried them to Roanoke. They asked me all kinds of questions. They asked me if I've ever gambled. I said "I gamble every morning I open those restaurant doors. Yes, I gamble, every day". He said "That's not what we meant." I said "I know what you meant". They asked if I've ever played cards. I said, "Yeah I've played some cards, but I make my living selling tacos, not playing cards." I reached into my pocket and pulled out about three thousand dollars that I had wrapped up in a rubber band. I took it out and sat it on the table in front of these two agents. I said "You see that money? I made that money. I paid taxes on that money and whatever the hell I do with that money, I have every right to do it."

They said, "Well maybe". I said, "There's no maybe". They always had a tape recorder going. One had a pad out and a pencil. This went on for two days. They asked me if I drank. I said "I have a social drink now and then but no I don't drink". I used to. Until I found out that it didn't do me any good. I actually hadn't really drank since I was 27 years old. I was 37 then. They finally said that it would take 90 days for them to complete their investigation and that they would get back to me then. They turned the tape recorder off. Put the pad and pencil back. I said "I have something I want to say". "Well just a minute", they said.

They turned the tape recorder back on. Got the pencil and pad back out. I told them that they could check from now until Hell freezes over and I for one knew that hell wasn't going to freeze over. I said, "You'll find out that Dave Flynn never cheated anyone out of anything, much less the government". They said, "Well if that's the case, you got nothing to worry about". I said "That's the case and I want you to understand, if I lose everything I got, everything, I will fight this until the dying end. I know I haven't done anything wrong!" Then I left.

Well, I fired that bookkeeper in Winchester because he wasn't any help. I took my stuff and left. I got another bookkeeper in Charlottesville. I finally got an accountant, which I should have done a long time ago. But I got an education in this audit that is unbelievable. They took all my records and they notified me that the statues of limitations was running out on '74 and would I sign a year's extension. That's how it was back then. I said "NO, I'm not giving you an extension. The balls in your court, bounce it!"

Well, they bounced it. They sent me a tax bill for 1974. We'd only been in business for 4 years. It was for 88 thousand dollars. A lot of it was a 10-thousand-dollar penalty and a lot of it was for interest. Katie almost had a stroke. I said "Don't worry about it. I know what they did. They took our receipts every day and our deposits and the checks we wrote every day and the difference between the two was over 220 some thousand dollars. The taxes was over 80 some thousand plus the penalty. That's what they had done. I was pretty sure of it.

So, I rented out another office spot, put out a banquet table. Got me an adding machine, a ledger sheet. They gave me my records back for 1974. I went over all the cash paid out on all the different locations. Anyway, I came out with 220 thousand dollars in cash pay outs. So, I called my attorney and told him. I told him I had the receipts and the ledger sheet. I never gave them that extension, but that's just what they had done. My attorney told me to meet him in his office. He had a tax attorney come in. He asked if the two of them could talk alone for a few minutes. I went outside. It was about 10 minutes, not too long. The other attorney came out. My attorney said, the attorney told him, "They are going to get you, because they know you've done something wrong". I knew I had done nothing wrong. I said, "They are not going to get me, unless they invent something up that I didn't do."

This audit went on for 3 years. Longer than 3 years. It started messing with my head. I would start to wonder if I'd be driving one day and see a little black car put their lights on to pull me over, and wonder if they threw in some dope or something in the back just to get me in trouble. Word got around that I was in trouble with the IRS. All the banks I dealt with. The purveyors I dealt with, didn't care because I paid them weekly. The banks I dealt with, one guy told me "Look, I believe you, I trust you and anything you need help with, let me know and we can see what we can help you with." The rest of the banks shunned me.

My attorney helped me get my court hearing relocated in Richmond, from Northern VA. He was going to send the ledger sheets, copies of the receipts and ask for a redetermination. A couple of agents came up from Richmond and asked to see all the receipts. I had everything they needed. I told Katie and Shelly to keep an eye on them to be sure they wouldn't take anything. The guys said "We're not going to do that". I said, "Hell, don't try to convince me. I've been going through a lot with you people." They asked me where I was going to be about 3:00 that day. I told them I would be at my restaurant across from Albemarle High School, in Charlottesville. They said they would look for me there about that time. They did. I said "Can I buy you guys a drink, a coke or something". They said "No". I said "Would you consider that a bribe?" They said, "No we have to get back onto Richmond". I said "Well what's the story?"

They said that there was a couple hundred dollars that they didn't understand. I said "Out of 220 thousand dollars, you don't understand a couple hundred"? They said "We know what we're doing". I said "Bull, you go on and make your report and we'll see where we're going from here".

Well after that, the attorney for the government got in touch with my attorney, and told us to come down there. We went. He was a little fat guy with a 3 piece suit on. Cocky. A typical government leach. He had this big stack of papers on me. He said, the position the government is going to take on 1974, as filed! This had nothing to do with 1975, '76, and they would soon be doing '77. He said it again. "It's considered filed"! I said, "You mean to tell me, I don't owe you 88 thousand dollars?" He said, "We're accepting it as filed". I leaned over his desk and stuck my finger close to his nose, and said "Thank you Jesus". He said "What?" I said, "Thank you Jesus". I said, "If you don't know who Jesus is, I'll tell you about Him." My attorney grabbed me by the arm and said "Come on Dave, lets get out of here".

Then they notified me that they wanted an extension on 1975 because the statues of limitation was running out on it. I learned what happened with all the stuff from 1974, so I granted the extension for 1975. I didn't want to go through all that again. It needed to be filed and settled in a 3-year period. It was 1978 by this time.

Not too long after that they called me and said that they wanted to return my stuff from the last 2 years to me. They wanted to meet me in my restaurant at 9:00 the next morning. They said to be there so they could return my stuff to me. I said, I wasn't sure I'd be able to meet them at that day and time. He said "Look, I'm telling you to be there". I told them that, "I was going to be where I wanted to be tomorrow at 9:00. That they had taken those records from me and that when they could bring them back and I could sign for them, I'll let you know where I'm going to be, but it isn't going to be at that restaurant at 9:00."

He interrupted me and told me to be at the restaurant at 9:00 tomorrow morning.

I said, "I'm telling you, to go to hell". And I hung up the phone. Katie was upset and thought they were going to come get me right then and take me off in handcuffs. I said, "They're not coming up and they won't do anything".

This went on for a week or two maybe. I'm in the restaurant in Harrisonburg. Katie calls me and tells me that they were there unloading the records and setting them on the floor. They told her that she had to sign for them. I said "He took them from me". I asked to put him on the phone. I knew that the other agent was with him. I told him that I was in Harrisonburg and I wasn't going to sign for these papers right then. That they took them from me, and at my convenience, I would sign for them.

He said, "Katie could sign for them. It didn't matter but they were not going to take them back with them."

I asked to have Katie put back on the phone. I told Katie, that her and Shelly were to grab their purses and go to lunch. Anywhere they wanted to go. To leave those two jokers standing there. One of the agents hollers "He's telling them to leave and go to lunch". Katie and Shelly left. The two agents were left standing there.

They finally got '74 and '75 down to where they said, I owed them 12 thousand dollars. My attorney said "For crying out loud, pay them."

I said "I don't owe them. They have to show me!" I showed them some mistakes they had made. This went on for a little while.

They told me that two agents from Roanoke was coming to talk to me. I thought it was the criminal investigators again. I said, "Sure, I'd talk to them". They came up. The head agent had the tax returns for '75 and '76. He said "We need to get this off the books" I said you still have '77. They weren't worried about '77 right then. They asked where I was going to be at 2:00. I said I could come back to the office. I sat across the desk from these two agents. '75 they said I owed 300 some dollars and for '76 I owned 290 something. Anyway, for the 2 years they said I owed about 600 dollars or so. I said "What's this?" They said that's what I owed and to pay it and we'll put this behind us. Now these guys had put me through 3 years of hell. This is that partner I took in back in 1970. Always getting his. He didn't care how he got it, or who he hurt getting it. So, I looked at that, and I said "I don't think so. If you can get it that close, you should be able to get it to 0". They said, "In '75 and '76 you filed your taxes on your income on the Charlottesville restaurant, on 50%. And your mother filed 50%. But you owned 51%... ...owned 49%. So in '75 and... going to get back, what you're go... ...laughed so hard.

I said "You're right". This was the first ti... ...at these guys and said they were right. I should have paid it on 51... ...were right this time. I called my attorney. He said "Write them a ch... ...aid "I don't think so". "What do you mean?" I said "I'll take care of it"... ...d and accepted both copies. We talked about ball games and a few ... things. The agents said "Well if you'll give us a check we'll get back on... ...oanoke. I said "I don't' think so". "What do you mean?" I said that I agreed ... the papers they gave me, and that I owed them 620 dollars but I told them t... I thought they were convinced that no matter what, everyone owed them. No matter how honest they are. Everyone owes them. I got an education on the last 3 years on taxes I'll never forget. I don't think I could have gone to college and gotten a better education on it. I will owe you from now on. I'm not paying estimated quarterlies and my taxes like I've done for the last 7 years. I'm going to file for an extension every year, so I don't have to pay it until October, which is legal. And then I'm going to send you about a third of what I owe you. Then I'll get it all paid before it's time to do taxes again. So, I'll let you all leave here today knowing that I owe you, because I'm damn sure, I'm going to owe you from now on. They said "Okay, if that's how you feel". They left.

I got my first bill for the 600 and some dollars. Mom got her return. I told Katie to only pay 100 dollars. They billed us again. They sent a nasty note, "Avoid a judgement against your bank account". I ignored all that crap. I told Katie to send them another check this time for 200 dollars. We got it paid, like I said, before the next tax season. This was now 1978. They didn't do 1977 like they said they were going to do. They didn't do '78. This is now 2023. They have never done another tax audit on me. Lord,

Dave Flynn

...e, but since 1977 they haven't done
I hope they don't ever d... ..., I hope they are ready for a fight. They
another one on me. If ... ...rong.
have to prove to me ...
... ...ting us through this time in our lives.
Thank you, Lor...

## CHAPTER 14

## Carl Silver

After this IRS audit, I started getting rid of the places that were not doing really well anymore. Like the two chili shops. I got rid of them. I had the one El Cabrito's up in Fredericksburg. It wasn't doing too well. I kept trying to get things going. I felt like people could steal faster than I could drive back then. The speed limit was 55 miles per hour. I had places all over the place. Amherst, Fredericksburg, Harrisonburg, Staunton. I was driving all the time. I wanted to do something about Frederiksberg. Carl Silver owned almost everything up in Fredericksburg. He was the king of development and had made himself quite an empire up there. I wanted an El Cabrito's up there. He had agreed to build on the location I wanted but I picked a bad location. The lease I had on that place was super thick. It would take a Philadelphia lawyer 3 weeks to analyze that thing. I didn't care. I was going to pay the rent. It was what I wanted. Carl built the building; we made the deal.

3 or 4 years later, so late '70s early '80s, I decided I needed to do something about this location. I was looking over the lease. One of the stipulations was that you couldn't close! I wanted to close this location for a while because I wanted to change things.

I went to talk to Carl. I told Carl that I wanted to buy the property from him instead of renting it. I wanted to do the deal then, but that I may not be able to do it in 60 to 90 days. I wanted to give him 240 thousand dollars. It was a corner lot. There was a parking lot around it. That parking lot was to be shared with the other shops around it as well. I told him that if he didn't do this deal with me, then he'd see a sign in the paper saying "Mexican Restaurant goes broke". I told him that he didn't want that and I didn't' want that. A week later he wanted me to give him 270 thousand for the place. I told him I couldn't do that. I told him I could give him 40 thousand down and for one year, if he could carry the rest, I'd get a bank to give me a note to pay off the rest. Honestly it was probably worth about 220 thousand or less. I had to think about it. He was set on 270! It was too much money. It wasn't worth that kind of money. It was priced too high. I told him I offered 240 because I thought that was a fair deal. He then said 260 but that was it! I had to think about it. I thought about it. "I can't do that I said! It's not worth it. Again, priced too high!"

He said "I buy wholesale and I sell retail". I understood, but I knew that I couldn't give him what he wanted. I decided to make him a deal. A gambling deal. A flipping a coin kind of a deal. You flip a coin, you call it. If it comes up the way you call it, I'll give you the 260. 40 down, 220 in a year. BUT, if it comes up in my favor, then I give you 220, same deal, 40 down and the rest of it within a year.

He looked at me and laughed. He said "You're serious". I said "I'm dead serious". I needed to get this behind me right then! He figured that if he flipped the coin, he would lose 20 thousand from what I was offering him in the first place. I said "Yeah but if you win, you'll make 20 thousand more than I offered you." He said he'd be better off just taking my offer of 240. 40 thousand down and the balance within a year! So that's the way we wrote it up and that's what we did.

In the meantime, I shut her down. I remodeled it, made it a full-service restaurant, and called it La Hacienda. I had a girl working for me in Charlottesville at the time. She was a good worker. Bonnie. I wanted to move her to this location. She agreed. It was doing pretty well. It was turning the bottom line. This went on for a while, until a new health inspector came in there and started driving Bonnie nuts.

When it was El Cabrito's, we had this one health inspector that just loved us and always said wonderful things about us. We always had a good report. It wasn't the case with this lady. I wanted to get this problem solved. We agreed to meet. She asked me to come up there and meet with her in the next day or so. She was "riding the horse". She wanted me to walk around the place with her so she could point out everything that needed to be dealt with. I had to follow her around the place like a dog following an owner or something. She pointed out different things. They were little. There was a storage room and I just had a light bulb in there. Just dry goods and paper goods. The current bulb was a 100 watt bulb. She wanted it to be a 150-watt bulb. She said it needed to have better visibility in that room. She asked to sit down to go over everything with me. I agreed but first wanted to grab something out of the office there. She said "Go ahead." I went into the office and grabbed the stack of the previous health inspections from the other guy. I showed her they all said "Good". "Excellent". I asked if that guy was still working. She said he was still working but in a different location. That he had his way of doing things and that she had her ways. She was younger and probably just out of college or something.

I said "Let me tell you something honey. I don't want to start something, but if you go next door to "Wood Grille" and take a bacteria sample, and if you can find something worse here at my place, than I'd be more than happy to follow you around, and hear what all you need me to do. Until you do that, though, I don't want you coming in here and bugging my manager Bonnie anymore. If you want to inspect this place, you give me a call and I'll come up here myself. Until then, you can go right on back to the health department because we are done for now."

She was all red faced and flustered but she left. 2 or 3 months later, we were getting ready to get a new health permit and they mailed ours! She never came back! I'm sure she had gone back to the health department and cried to her boss about what I had said. We always had a good rating. After that, we never saw another health inspector at that place again.

After a little while I decided to sell the place. It never did end up doing that great. It was okay but not like I wanted it to be. I found a guy that had a Dairy Queen franchise. He liked it. He couldn't buy it, but he'd rent it from me. We agreed to a 5-year lease. He would pay the rent every month, and after 5 years, whatever the tax appraisal was, he would give me that and 10 percent above whatever the appraisal came back to be. If he would do that, it would be his. He agreed. He was paying more rent than what the monthly payment was on it. That's how I was able to get away from that deal.

Thank you, God, for this time in our lives.

# CHAPTER 15

# Lupos and Hilltop Grocery

I HAD A FRIEND IN CHARLOTTESVILLE THAT HAD A PIZZA AND HOAGIE shop next door to my restaurant. It was called Lupos. He was being robbed blind by his brother in law and sister. I tried to tell him but he didn't listen to me. Eventually he went bankrupt. Well I got it in my head, to see if I could get in touch with the owner of that place, and try to get a lease on that property. It was a nice business. A goldmine. He was busy. It was next to the University. I talked to the owner of the property and he said "Sure", as long as he was getting the same rent as he had been. I don't remember now what that was. It wasn't a small amount. I wanted to go to the bankrupt court and buy everything in the place. They still had to appraise everything, etc. I offered them 5 thousand dollars for everything. I was currently leasing the property. I got it. I had this nice place. Drive through window. Sold pizzas and hoagies. As long as you had people in there you could trust, there's no way you couldn't make money! It was a good deal.

Anyway, I had a plumber friend. He was a "hoss of a man". He was in his 50s and he could drop down and give you 50 push ups like it was nothing! He had a wife named Martha. She was crazy about him. She would do anything in the world to help him. She had 2 kids by her first husband. Sometimes they would help me in the restaurant. Odie, was my plumber friend, and I wanted to make him a deal. I needed someone to run it, and watch over it. I wanted Martha to help him in there too. I said I'd do all the bookwork at the office. Hire all the people, etc. We were "knocking it out". I made my 5 thousand dollars back. He was making a good living. We were doing really well. It didn't take much time at all.

In the meantime, over across from Albemarle High School, the El Cabrito's had a country store next to it, called "Hilltop". It was owned by 2 brothers. It was a nice place. Stocked well. The brothers decided they wanted to sell it. I offered to buy it from them for 125 thousand dollars. It had lots of stock in it too. Beside it was a little barber shop. He paid rent to me. I had to pay the 2 brothers the rent.

I didn't really want to bother much with the store, so I asked this guy that used to work for me at Kenny Burger if he'd be interested in this. He loved the idea but couldn't get the money to buy it. He was interested in running it though. I said "I'll come up with the money, you draw a salary, pay me my ½ off, and we'll split everything." I thought we'd do alright. He loved the idea. I did tell him one thing though, I didn't want to sell wrapping paper, and all this scented stuff. Different stuff that kids use to smoke marijuana. He agreed.

We were opened about 3 or 4 months, maybe longer at this point. I went in there one day to look around, and check on things. There was this large display of wrapping paper. Scented. Every kind of wrapping paper you could think of! I didn't want any part of all that. He said there was a big market for all that stuff and that we were making a lot of money on that stuff. I didn't care how much we were making. I didn't want it or need it! I told him that in the beginning! I wanted that stuff out of there.

I gave him a week to get rid of it. I came back about 2 weeks later. I went into the store. Store was well stocked, it was busy. Kids from across the street, it was doing really well. The wrapping paper was still there though. He didn't get rid of it. I got a big trash can and scooped all those papers into it. He got upset and said "What are you doing?" I said "I'm doing what I said I was going to do, if you didn't take care of it." I told him that he could throw it in the dumpster if he wanted or do whatever, but he was no longer going to sell that in that store! He agreed. That was the end of the smoking papers being sold across from the high school.

Odie's wife, ended up drowning one night. She was drunk and swam out too far. That was hard on the family after that. Odie started questioning me about the books and how I was running things between the two restaurants. He thought maybe I was buying stuff for one business and billing it to the other business. I couldn't believe he would think such a thing! He had an attorney who was talking to him about this. I told Odie to give me a "buy /sell" agreement. Anything he was willing to give me, and anything he was willing to take and walk away with. He and his attorney talked. They thought the business was probably worth, 40 thousand dollars. He said he'd give 20 or take 20. I said "Good enough". I had enough other things going on at the time. He came up with the money and gave me 20 thousand dollars. That was my ½ of it.

3 or 4 months later Odie decided to sell the place. He was asking 40 thousand for it. Meanwhile the guy who was running the store, said he wanted to get into that Lupos restaurant. He said "Lets buy it". He wanted me to go in with him. He wanted to keep an eye on the store and run the restaurant too. I told him I didn't think it was a very good idea. He kept whining about it.

Finally one day, I told him to tell Odie he'd give him 20 thousand dollars for the place. He laughed and said that Odie would "throw him out the window." I said "No he won't". I knew that Odie would say, "Does Dave have anything to do with this?" I told him, to tell Odie "Yes".

Odie said "Can't you do better than that?" Odie knew that I was involved. Odie knew that I would pay him! We ended up coming up with a deal of 10 thousand right then, and then another 10 thousand in 6 months. I didn't want any trouble with anyone. The store wasn't doing all that great once my friend came over to Lupos. I didn't want the store anymore. I told my friend to take the store, and I'd take the restaurant. Or that he could take the restaurant and I'd take the store. My friend ended up taking Lupos and I got the store. I sold the store for 120 thousand dollars. I was able to get out from being the middle guy with the rent and lease too.

My friend called me one day, and said he was in West Virginia. He said he wasn't coming back to work. I said, "What are you going to do about Lupos?" He said "I'll sell it back to you. Whatever you think is a fair price".

I told my friend that I'd give him 10 thousand dollars for his half. He agreed to take it. Now I got the restaurant back. I didn't have the time to run it like it should have been run. I tried putting in different people. One guy was a good cook, his wife had Polio, she was in a wheelchair. They had a son together. He was working in Lupos for me. This would end up being the family I'd use in my next chapter.

Thank you, God, for this time in our lives.

# CHAPTER 16

# Family Restaurant

I moved this family to Amherst. Got them all set up with a little place and everything. He was going to run this restaurant for me. It was going to be alright, as long as he was honest with me. I had given him a good deal. I told him we can only make money here! He was happy for this opportunity! I told him not to steal from me. I let him know that I'd catch him, if he started stealing from me. I told him this in the beginning. I told him it would always show up if anything went missing. He promised me he would never do such a thing.

So, I had the restaurant in Lynchburg, one in Amherst, Harrisonburg, Charlottesville, Fredericksburg. I had 7 or 8 of them at one time. Most of the time, 3 or 4 of them was carrying the other 3 or 4. I would go down to Lynchburg once or twice a month. On my way, I'd stop into the Amherst location, to see how things were going. I'd take a reading on the register, and when no one else was looking or around, I'd take 20 dollars out of my pocket and put it in the register. I knew that he had daily check in sheets, and he had to keep track of the money that was in the register. I knew that if he was doing the job right, that this register would be at least 20 dollars over, if not more, if he was selling some to go items and not putting in the tickets or something. So anyway, when I got the check in sheets at the office, the 20 dollars didn't show up. It would be within a dollar one way or the other, all the time.

I decided the next time I went out there, I would put 27 dollars in the register. I did. That didn't check out either. Whatever he had extra, he'd pocket the cash. He didn't know what he was "doing wrong", he was just happy he had extra and he kept it. Stole it. The third time I went by, instead of putting a 20-dollar bill in the register, I took a 20 out of it. The books showed only a dollar or so short. He hadn't been working for me for too long at this point. I told him I wanted to see him at the office and I showed him the 3 check in sheets.

I told him what I had been doing with the register and I asked him why he wasn't checking it on the daily sheets. The moral of the story was that on the third time, he should have been 20 dollars short, but he wasn't. I reminded him that if he was stealing from me, I'd catch him. He shook his head and said "He'd make it up to me". I said "No, you're not going to make it up to me. You're going to move yourself back to Charlottesville, because I'm not going to pay the rent on your place anymore. Take your wife and your son and know that I trusted the wrong individual." He left. He went back to Charlottesville.

Then I found a man and his wife in Amherst to run the place. She was a good operator. It worked out fine. They did well for a while, but what little bit of money I was making on this place wasn't really worth me to keep it. I made him and her an offer for them to take it over and make it theirs. I don't remember what it was. I know it wasn't a lot, but they agreed to it. To the best of my recollection after 10 or 15 years, they were still running it. So it was a good deal for them, and it was certainly a good deal for me, because I got rid of that headache.

Thank you, God, for this time in our lives.

# CHAPTER 17

# Unemployment Commission

My "partner", once again felt he needed more. You paid a percent of what your payroll was every month to the Unemployment Commission. I had the lowest rate you could possibly get. Very low for a restaurant business. I paid 1/10$^{th}$ of 1 percent. Some people had to pay 3 ½ clear on up to 7 or 8 percent, because they had a big turn over and things like that. People would draw unemployment so your rate was based on your record.

The place back in Charlottesville, called Lupos, that I had taken back; I only had it maybe 6 months, when we got a bill. In that location my bill was raised to 3 percent! All the other locations had stayed the same. I told Katie not to pay that! I said to pay what we always had paid. 1/10$^{th}$ of 1 percent.

Someone I knew from the Unemployment Commission came to see me about this. Nice guy, I knew him. He said "Dave, you can't do that". I said, "I earned that rate!" He said "You sold the business and there are people drawing unemployment." I said, "I don't care and I'm not paying that rate." The only other way I was going to pay this, was if I was standing in front of a judge and if they told me I had to pay it! He said "Alright. I'll turn it in". They turned it in to some other guy in charge. He was in Harrisonburg. He said "You'll just have to pay it". I said "For crying out loud, what does it take to get it through you people's head? I'm not paying that! The only way I'll pay it, is if a judge forces me to." He said "Alright". Then he turned it into the next guy in command. He was in Fredericksburg. I got letters. Phone calls. "You're violating the Unemployment Commissions rules and to avoid any more penalties, you need to pay this bill."

He just wanted to get this straight but I told him once again, "I AM NOT PAYING IT. It's just that simple." I had several businesses. I had been in business for 12 years at this time and I had never had anyone drawing unemployment.

Then I got a call from an agent in Richmond saying that as long as I paid what was owed on the back, they wouldn't give me a penalty. They said let's just get this behind us. I again told them I wasn't going to pay that rate. I had earned the other rate, and that was the only rate I was going to pay.

He said "Well looks to me like we're going to take you to court." I said, "Fine, I want to hear a judge tell me after all these years of business with an excellent record, that I needed to start paying a higher rate." Better yet, I wanted to talk to the head guy in charge. The head of the Unemployment Commission was located in Richmond. I drove to Richmond in the rain! He thought we'd be able to work this out. I said "The only way this is going to work out is if you give me the rate I have always been paying".

I got to see the head of commissions guy. I was in his office. Dark hair, 3-piece suit. Good looking guy. He was in la la land. I told him that I had been in business for 12 years, and had never had anyone drawing off me.

I was out of this location for 6 or 7 months, and during that time someone else had taken over the business. I told him that it wasn't under me, that this had happened. I wasn't going to pay that bill when it was someone else's doing. They basically told me that the rules were "in the book". That they could go to jail if they didn't follow the rules and so could I. I told him that I didn't think he even knew what that book said! At this point, I was willing to get the TV station, the radio stations, and others involved because I was so fed up. It wasn't fair and this was crazy to me. I told him I would let the news media know what they were trying to do to me and that they were borrowing money from other departments to keep the Commission afloat and that was illegal.

Finally, he said "There's got to be something we can do for him".

Basically, they were able to work around this and "take care of it". I was to escrow ½ the payroll and let the other ½ go with the business. Then when I took back the business, I had to show the escrow payroll and I'd be "entitled" to the same rate. If I did that, I'd be able to "work it all out". That was all I wanted.

I was glad they were able to work this out for me! HA! Bunch of crooks!

I got what I wanted. That's it. The local agent wanted to know how things worked out and I told him. He said, "Well that's illegal." I said, "Well, why don't you go to Richmond and tell them that?" He said, "No". He planned to retire in a couple of years and he did not want any trouble.

Thank you, God, for getting us through that time in our lives.

# CHAPTER 18

# Change Sign

Let's get back to Lupos. After I had taken it back, I felt like it wasn't doing as well as it should or could be doing. I got it in my head to change the sign and fix a few things. I wanted to call it Pappy's Fried Chicken. I wanted to still serve the pizza and the hoagies and I wanted to include delivery. I bought 3 postal jeeps for delivery. I had guys driving these jeeps. We had a certain boundary we would stay in. We were busy. It was a good idea.

Well, when I got it in my mind to do this, I wanted to change the sign. The rules had changed for the size of the signs by this time. I wanted to have a big sign like I had at La Hacienda. Well, "they" had told me I had to have a certain size and that was the limit. It was smaller than what I wanted. I didn't like that.

So, I went down to the county office building to see the guy in charge of this sign. He was sharp enough. He had a big position. I told him what I wanted to do with this sign. I had a diagram drawn up. I wanted to take the big sign down and put up another sign that was about 20 % of that one, but I also wanted an "action" sign put up under that new one, so that made it about 30 % of the old sign. They said "Well, why can't you just do the sign and we'll get that passed, but not do the action sign?" I said I didn't want to do that, because I wanted to have a few special things on that action sign.

I asked him to meet me at the place where the sign would go, so that I could show him. He agreed and we set up a time the next day to meet. The huge Lupo sign, I was going to take down, and the lighting up at the top of the building. I wanted to take the whole thing down. I don't think he liked the idea much. He said he needed to talk to another guy about this. In the end, they agreed to let me do it! I was shocked! I said "What? You're going to let me do this?" He said "Yeah". I was getting what I wanted but I was aggravated because he had said "We'll let you do it". Even if it was "wrong". So, I turned and walked away.

Anyway, I got the sign up the way I wanted it. It wasn't a good move. I would have been better off if I would have kept it the way it was, and got a smart operator in that place. It was so hard to find a decent operator. Everyone wanted to steal off me.

Speaking of that, I had this problem in Staunton. The manager was stealing me blind. I bought big blocks of Swiss cheese and we grated it up for the Mexican food. Well, when we got the bill at the office for this cheese, it always looked to me like we were using less cheese than what we were buying. There was a motel next to the restaurant. I sat up and watched what was happening. I was watching the unloading of the cheese. Everything looked ok. I went in there and counted the boxes of cheese. Everything looked ok. I went in a few days later and counted again. Everything looked right. Finally, this got to bothering me so much, that I called the distributor. I told him that I was paying for a lot more cheese than I was using. I told him that someone was stealing off of me, and I couldn't catch them.

The moral of the story is, the distributor told me that a lot of times the manager of this location would come and pick up a few boxes of the cheese in his own car. I finally caught him. I was paying 50 cents a pound, or so, for this cheese and this guy was selling it for 25 cents a pound to these country grocery stores. He sold a lot of it and I had to let him go. I never prosecuted him. I never prosecuted anyone and I've caught a lot of people stealing from me over the years. Anyway, that's the story about the cheese ordeal.

Thank you, God, for getting us through this time in our lives.

# CHAPTER 19

# Bad Checks

So, the chicken thing didn't end up working out really well. I wanted to get out of it but the landlord wouldn't let me out of the lease. I was his bread and butter.

Anyway, this pizza outfit, a national chain, not one that is popular right now, he came along and wanted to rent it. He wanted to open up a franchise store there. Him and his friend. His friend sold equipment. New and used equipment. And the other guy owned burger places. He owned about 4 or 5 of them. So, I figured this was a pretty good group to deal with.

We made a deal. I basically just told him that I needed the rent to be paid. They were to send me a check every month for the rent. Then I would pay the landlord because he wouldn't let me off the lease. Well, they got all remodeled and opened up and the first check I got, wasn't any good. So, I called his partner, who I knew better than the other guy and he said "That's okay, just run it again and again". I said "Look, I paid this rent, I'm not in this thing to see that you people stay in business, I got to have the rent money." He said "I'll get it straightened out". Well, this went on a couple more months and suddenly, I get another bad check. Well, this really upset me. I got all over him about it and the guy from the burger place called me and he said he put the money in there and to run the check again. This really upset me. I said "I can't have you continue to do this! You all pay the rent, and pay it on time or we're going to have a problem." He said "Look I've been in business for a long time, and I have all these burger places I said "I don't care how long you've been in business, it's my business to pay this rent, but I can't pay it, unless you pay me." He said "It will be there". Well, it was. Until the next month, when it wasn't good again.

Well, all hell flew into me, and I went down to the nearest hardware store and picked up a piece of chain and a lock. I took them down to the pizza shop and put the chain through the two front doors and put the lock on it. This was about 9:30 in the morning or something. I Went back next door to my restaurant I had there. Before I knew it, the manager from the pizza shop came running through my back door saying "What are you doing? You can't do that!" I said "What do you mean what am I doing?" I said, "You see this check, it's not any good! Until you make it good, meaning cash or money order, you're not opening, it's just that simple."

He said "You can't do that". I said "I thought I just did". He left and went next door. Next thing I knew, his partner calls me. He went off. He said "We can sue the hell out of you and when all is said and done, you won't have anything left. Won't have to worry about paying the rent."

I said, "Then that's what you need to do, because I have a lot of bad checks here that you all have made good, but you haven't made this one good yet, and until you do make it good, you're not opening! I don't mind going before a judge and telling him why this happened." He hung up the phone.

The next thing I knew, I got a call from his attorney. His attorney really went down on me. He said "You won't be able to afford to buy a pencil". He went on and on. Once he was done, I said "The only way you all will get that chain off the door, is if I get my money and start getting it on time. Otherwise, I'll chain it up again. If you're going to sue me, then sue me." Then I hung up.

Five minutes later my attorney called me, because their attorney called him and he told me that I couldn't do that. His name was Bosley Crowther. I said "Bosley, don't tell me I can't do that. I've already done it! Until I get paid, they are not opening, it's just that simple."

He said "Let's get them opened and then we'll get it straightened out." I said again, "No, until they pay me, they are not opening and it's that simple." He hung up. Called back a few minutes later and said "You can't get the money by 11:00 but it would most likely be there a little after 11:00. Maybe 11:15." Their attorney was going to send me a check from their escrow account.

Well, I was smart enough and had dealings with attorneys over the years and I knew that you don't write a check from your escrow account unless it's good. He said from then on, that the rent would be paid from his office! I said "Good enough!" So, he told me to open the doors! I said "That check better be coming and it better be good". I opened the doors about 11:20 that morning.

A few minutes later, here comes an attorney from Waynesboro with a check from his escrow account. She said "We're sorry for what happened. From now on, we'll see to it that you get paid". I was pleased with this.

Well, they didn't do well. They were going under. The restaurant next to me. A little while later these Chinese people wanted to take it over. It was a good spot, right there next to the Coliseum. They told me that they would take the rent over and pay me. They had talked to the landlord. I said "If the landlord is happy with that, then he should be happy taking the rent directly from you."

It ended up all working out. I got in touch with the guy that owned the property, and he said that he had a chance to make even more money off the rent than he was currently getting. So, he wanted to take this deal from them. However, he wanted to be sure that they would pay him for about 6 months to a year. If they paid him, then he would let me out of the lease. I said "No, we're not going to do that." I wanted to get the check from them, keep the difference and pay him what I owed him. He said, "I believe these people will pay". I said, "Then you let me out of this lease and you deal directly with them." He thought about it and that is just what he did. I no longer had to worry about it!

Thank you, God, for getting us through this time in our lives.

# CHAPTER 20

# Taxes

To get back to the Government a little bit, like I said before, they've always got their hand in your pocket. They're always going to get "theirs". In the restaurant business, there were 17 different taxes. They all had to be paid, sales tax, utility tax, gasoline tax, liquor license tax, and then tax on your liquor. 17 different ways to make money off of that check. I had to think about all that and include all that in the bill I gave each customer that came in to eat with me. Then they came up with this meal tax. They tried this in the city back in the early 80's I guess it was. I started an organization called "S.M.A.R.T" That stands for: Sensible. Modest And Reasonable Taxes. "Vote no to meals tax". I had that slogan put on a business card. I got almost every restaurant owner in Charlottesville to join in paying for advertisement to oppose that tax. It kept it out for 2 years. It wasn't put on a vote for the people. It was the city councils right to put it in by majority vote. So that's what they did. So, then we had a meals tax added to all the other stuff.

Well, I got it in my head I wasn't going to pay this tax. I put big signs up in my windows "NO MEALS TAX HERE!" When the people came in, I didn't charge them that. That went on for about 2 or 3 months, until the attorney from the city came to see me and told me that I couldn't do that. I said "I am doing it. It's an unfair tax". I said that I was going to fight this until the dire end. He said "Well, you can't win. You might as well pay it." I said "That is nothing but a poor man's tax. Another way to get people without, to give more to the people with." I wasn't going along with it.

He said "Well, you don't leave me any choice but to send you a court order, take you to court, and they'll make you pay it." Well, I got a lot of publicity out of it. I was in the TV, on the radio, in the newspaper. Pictures of the place and pictures of me saying "It's just a poor man's tax." I know they have it everywhere anymore. It's just another way to tax the poor man. I had to go to court over this. The city attorney was giving his side to the judge. I owed about 4- or 5-months' worth of back taxes on the meals tax. The Judge said to me, "Mr. Flynn, do you have an attorney?" I said "No, but I guess I need one." He said, "Yeah I think you need one too." He said that we would put this off for 30 more days and then I'd come back in there with my attorney and we'll see if we can get this thing resolved. I agreed and left. I didn't think I would win. So, I never got an attorney, and again, it's been about 5 months at this time, and I still owed all that meal tax. I wasn't collecting any meals tax from the customers. It was 3 percent or something like that. I fought my own case. I didn't think I was going to win, but I was willing to try. I thought I had a good case.

The Judge asked me "How much business do you think you do a month?" I said, "About 30 or 40 thousand". He said, "So you round it off about 30 thousand, that'd be about 6 months, so that would be around 180 thousand dollars". He said "Three percent of that…" I said "Well wait a minute Your honor! If we're going to be fair about this, I admit that I haven't paid this tax. But I also haven't been collecting this tax either!" I never took the meals tax! So, for him to come up with a figure for me to have to pay wasn't fair on something I hadn't even been collecting in the first place. He listened to my case! Meanwhile the city attorney was over there doing his "war dance". He wanted me to pay every penny of what they said I owed. Judge agreed that if I hadn't been collecting it in the first place, I didn't owe it.

He said "Well let's just say 30 thousand dollars at 3 percent is about 9 hundred dollars for this past month. Will you agree to pay that? Then you need to start to pay it from now on. If you'll agree to this, we can go from there. Case closed!" Down the hammer went! The city attorney was so upset about this! That was a cheap way out of that! Lord have mercy! I had so many people on my side. When I finally had to start paying that tax, I knew that it was time for me to get out of the city. We moved the business up to Pantops!

Thank you, God, for getting us through that time in our lives.

# CHAPTER 21

# Real Estate and Auctioneers License

In the early 80's I went into the real estate business. I got a real estate license. It wasn't easy. I'm not the sharpest person you give a pencil to, when I try to take a test. I went to Richmond and took the test. Failed it. They told me not to worry about it. To come back in 6 months and take it again. I knew that in 6 months I wouldn't be any faster. I couldn't finish the test in the time they gave me to take it. I knew all the answers. I just couldn't read it and put down the right mark on the test. The guy said "Well that's the rule". I said "I understand you've got another rule. I understand that you can take the test orally". That was correct. Someone could read the questions out loud and take the test that way. Well, that's just what I did. I answered the questions and aced the test! I got my real estate license just like that!

So, with my real estate license I got it in my head to make a deal with my brother-in-law, that was down in Florida. He's an excellent carpenter. I said to him, "You come up here to Virginia and you can come work with me. We'll build these spec houses and sell them." I had the real estate license so I could buy lots and I had the credit enough to get the financing depending on the price range of the lot. At the time, the houses we were building were only about 90 thousand dollars. I could buy the lots at Lake Monticello for 2 thousand dollars apiece, or 1500 dollars for some of them! So that's what we did.

We started building the houses and selling them. I never would let there be more than 3 of the houses on the ground at a time. If I had to take a lot less money on the sale of one of the houses to keep the crew on, that's just what I did. I made money on all of them though. I guess we built about 70 homes in Lake Monticello. All total we built over 90 homes.

I got it in my head then, that I wanted to get my auctioneer's license. So, I called down to Richmond to apply to get that license. The lady on the phone asked me what school I had been too. That they required me to have a certificate from a school saying I had been to an auctioneer's school. I said I didn't have all that, but that I had experience. She asked where. I told her Kentucky. She said "Do you have a license from Kentucky?" I told her, it wasn't required to have a license and that I didn't have one. She said "All I can tell you, is that if you don't have a certificate from a school, or some sort of experience to prove it, I can't do anything for you." I said "Experience?!"

Here I was on the phone with the girl and all of a sudden, I stared rattling off in my auctioneer's voice "You got a 40-dollar bid, now 45, 50 dollars. 60! Someone want to give me 65?" I was talking really fast like the auctioneer's talk! She said "Good enough. Send 75 dollars to us". That's just what I did. I got my license. I had it for 35 years or more.

Thank you, God, for this time in our lives.

## CHAPTER 22

# Contractors Class A Building License

I HAVE DONE A LOT OF AUCTIONS OVER THE YEARS. MOSTLY CHARITY auctions. I had done some restaurant and grocery liquidation, stuff like that. Dealing with people and places that I knew what the equipment was and how much to try to get for it. I didn't really go into it to where I was going to make a living being an auctioneer, but it was a trade I liked and picked up and did it for a time.

The building end of it, I had several purveyors I dealt with. It didn't make a difference what I wanted, when I wanted it, they would get it to me and get it where I wanted it!

Again, we're getting into the governments hand in this. You had the business license people coming in to see what you were doing right and what you were doing wrong. Most of these people had not even been working in the field that long. Every now and then you'd be fortunate enough to get someone who had been. We had a good reputation, especially in Fluvanna County, with the building inspector. In Albemarle

County, they had a bunch of building inspectors. There was this one, in Albemarle, we were building a house in Woods Edge. It was a big house on 10 acres of land. It was 20 acres, but I sold 10 of it to a neighbor there.

We were ready to pour the footers the next day. They were all dug and everything. There were metal stakes all around where the concrete had to go up to. We had about 5 more stakes to put into the ground. Up rolls this guy in a truck. He said "I see you're not ready yet?" I said, "We're almost done, you can go ahead and by the time you get over here, we'll be done". He goes "Naa, I'll just come back tomorrow!" I said "We got the concrete coming in the morning." He said "It doesn't make a difference, you can call and cancel that, because you don't have the okay on this yet". He told me he'd be back in the morning. He was an arrogant little cuss. He left.

Side note, my brother-in-law, who was the head carpenter on this project, had 30 years of experience and he had other guys with him who had 20 years of experience. Using all their experience, when I applied for the Class A building license, I used a business name and put these guys down as the officers. We got it just like that, because of all their experience. I didn't really have any experience, except in making money.

Anyway, to get back to this guy I was telling you about. He came out the next day on the building site. The concrete truck was there ready to pour the concrete. There was also a truck down the hill drilling the well for the house. I saw the building inspector watching the well being built. I went up to him and asked "Do you inspect wells too?" He said, "No". I asked him what he was doing then, because he didn't have 10 minutes the day before to wait as we finished up putting stakes in the ground, but he had all the time in the world as he was watching this well being dug. I told him I was going to call his boss and let him know this. I did. I didn't care if I had to wait a day or two until I had another building inspector come, but that I wasn't going to be dealing with this guy ever again. They said "Fair enough". That was the story about that guy.

There was this other time, we were building a custom home in Scottsville for this older couple I used to go to church with. She was "a piece of work" but I won't get into the details about all that. He was a nice guy. She was nice too, but she was in a wheelchair so I had to put in a handicap bathroom in there. Well, I knew what the requirements were. It had a basement, but under the bathroom, there had to be extra support. I had double floor joints in it, and at each corner of the bathroom I had an extra 4 x 4 post in the basement floor and to the bathroom.

I had a tile man that was ready to lay the tile, and there was a drain in the middle of the bathroom, where all the water could run down this one drain in the middle. I had to have it inspected before the tile could be laid. Here came the inspector, not the same guy, I was telling you about before! Another guy. He looked around and said "Well, I think you need to put more support in this". I said "You think?" I was shocked. I told him about the double support and all the 4 x 4 posts. He said "I think you need to put 6 x 6-inch posts in instead". I said "I could drive my pickup truck over this floor and these wouldn't budge". He told me until I enforced it better, he wasn't going to give me the okay.

I called the inspectors office. Couldn't get the head guy on the phone. So, I went to see him in person. He said "What's your trouble now?" I told him. He said "Well, maybe it needs more support". I said "Maybe it does, but it doesn't! I've done it the way it's supposed to be done. Haven't you got anybody here who's been working for more than 2 years who can come inspect this house?" By this time there was an older fellow who came in from the back, and he called him by name and said "Could you do me a favor in the morning, and go down to the job Flynn has going on, and check this support?" He said "Sure". I said I'd meet him there in the morning the next day. I was thankful to have someone who knew what they were doing come check things out.

He went to the bathroom and checked it all out. Went down in the basement and checked it all out. He said it was all okay and that he would pass it. I said "Thanks. I appreciate it". There was just so many of these young guys that came in there with their little white book and their authority and they wanted to push you around. I don't want to sound arrogant about it, but I'm not the type of guy that gets pushed. I ended up doing most of my building in Fluvanna County because of this type of thing. Albemarle county just had a different way of doing things. They were not the easiest place to do business with.

Thank you, God, for getting us through this time in our lives.

# CHAPTER 23

# 1985

You know it's kind of funny how a lot of people think. I had all these restaurant businesses going, the construction business, the real estate sales, and I was doing pretty well for myself. In the mid 80's, 1985 to be exact, I was at my restaurant in Staunton one day. The guy that owned the motel next door to the restaurant came trotting over like he always did, and said to me "You're not doing so well are you, Dave?" I said "What?" He said "Well, business is just not what it was, you're not doing as well as you were." I said "Well it could be better, but one gets down I got another one to pick it back up." He said "Oh, is that right?". He was kind of negative. The type of guy that thinks everyone is doing bad in life just because he was doing bad.

I had Katie with me. On the way back from Staunton, we stopped at Waynesboro at a Cadillac dealership there. We were both dressed in plain clothes. Nothing special. Nothing fancy. Comfortable, casual clothes. We got out and walked around for a bit. In the showroom, they had a pretty 1985 Cadillac. It was called "Heather", the color. Some people said it was purple. Some called it a "pimp automobile" but it was just a pretty Cadillac, really. I liked it. Katie liked it. The salesman there came up to us and said "Can I help you?" I said "Yes, I'd like to try this car out". He said "Well, do you have something you'd like to trade in?" I said "I haven't said anything about trading anything in, I just wanted to try out this car. Can I try it or not?"

He said "Well yeah, but would you like to fill out a credit application or something?" I said "No, I just want to try the car." He saw that I was getting pretty frustrated, so he made arrangements to get the car out of the showroom so we could try it out. I knew how much the car cost, because it had a sticker in the window with the price tag on it. I liked it. Katie liked it. We drove it. We got back to the dealership. I told the guy I wanted to buy it. He said "Would you like to talk to the sales manager? Maybe he could help with this?" I said "Fine". Sales manager came out, and said "How can we help you with this?" I said "I'd like to buy this car." I told him that I had a figure written down on a piece of paper, and that if they came close to that figure, I would buy the car. He said "Well, what price did you have in mind? Did you want to trade something in?" I said, "I'm not trading anything in." I told him that what I couldn't pay for, I could get. I told him to go work out the numbers. They went to the back for a bit. When they came back, they had a piece of paper with them. I looked at it and said "You know that's amazing. You are within 300 dollars of what I was willing to give for this car. I think that's close enough. I'm going to take it". He asked how I was going to pay for it. I asked if the owner of the dealership was there. He came out of his office and I introduced myself to him. He shook my hand. He knew who I was. He told me that I had some nice restaurants. I said "Yeah, they're alright. A lot of times one is carrying another one, but they do okay. Keeps my head above the water." He said "What can I do for you?"

I told him that I wanted to buy the car. That I could write him a check right then for everything but 5 thousand dollars. I told him to hold the title on it for 60 days and that I'd bring the rest of the money to him by then. I just wanted to take the car with me right then. I only owed 5 thousand more dollars on it. He told me, "You don't need to do that. I trust you." He told the guys to get it ready for me. In 60 days, I brought him the balance of the money I owed him. The moral of this story is: When I was back in Staunton in that Cadillac, the guy that owned that motel next to my restaurant, saw me in the new car. He said "Lord, everything is going pretty well for you, huh?" I said "Yeah. I'm doing alright." But the moral is that I wasn't doing any better that day, then when I had met with him a few weeks prior. It just looked to him like I was doing better. That's how people think.

I had a lot of trouble in Staunton. I had a guy work for me, he was a crackerjack cook. You could not stick him. We could seat 250 people just in the main dining room. We had another room in the back we could seat people in. We were opened 24 hours, Friday and Saturday. There were lots of dances around the area. I had another guy working for me, who worked the register and helped to handle some of the drunks that came in there. This one time there was a party of 6 that came in, and we didn't pull tables together. You waited until there was a table big enough to seat everyone. The guy in the party got upset and said "There's 2 tables right over there, why can't you just pull those two together?". He said, "We don't do that". Well 4 of the people in the party went and sat down at a table. All of a sudden, one of the guys grabs another table and starts to pull it to their table to put them together. He come over and moved the table back where it was supposed to go. He said "These are different stations, different girls are waiting on each station, and this table stays over here. Your girl is not waiting on that station over there."

The guy said, "I'm from New Jersey and I've never heard of such a thing. In New Jersey people accommodate you and have a desire to give you what you want." He pointed to the line of people waiting to be seated, at least 12 of them. He said "You're not in New Jersey, you're in Staunton. You 4 can sit here and eat but the other 2 need to wait for a table to open up, like all the rest of the people waiting." He was mad and he got up and left. That's how we could operate. We were so busy all the time, we were not going to let people be nasty to us and push as around. We weren't nasty to them, but we ran it that way and that was that.

One of the things I could not stand was when people were disrespectful to waitresses. My mother was a waitress when I was a child. She was also a waitress in our business. Well, one night a guy came into the restaurant. I knew who he was. He was the manager of a steak place on Afton Mountain. There was another guy with him. He was an arrogant cuss. Big guy. He was always touching all over the waitresses, grabbing them by the hip or the leg. He never kept his hands off them. The girls didn't like this. I overheard them say to each other, "You take him". "No will you please take him tonight?" I asked them what the issue was. They told me about this friend of his and what he did / how he acted with the ladies. I told them to go ahead and wait on him and I'd be watching. Sure enough, he grabbed the girl by the hip and squeezed her leg a little bit. I walked over and said that I needed to have a word with him. I asked him "Who do you think you are? Don't you know that this is someone's mother, or sister and she needs to be treated like a lady. He said "What are you talking about? I didn't hurt her." I said, "You're done and you're not going to do that anymore to anyone around here again." They got up and they left.

A few weeks later, I went into a restaurant in Charlottesville. A friend of mine named George owned it. They had a nice lounge. It was a nice place. George always liked me. He said "Let me buy you a drink. Sit down." He asked me how things were going. I told him, "Things were alright." All of a sudden, another guy walked in and sat down next to him. My friend, George looked right at the guy and said "I don't recall me inviting you to sit here. I'm having a drink with a friend of mine." He got up quickly and said "Sorry Boss". The boy left. This tickled me.

I was playing cards one night. This boy who worked for George came in to play cards too. He was known as the VIP of the restaurants. He was a nice-looking guy. He got a little mouthy. He had been drinking a little too much. He got an attitude. I knew he worked for George. He started running his mouth, about George and us and said he was just here to play cards. I said "Now, wait a minute young man. You're a little out of line here don't you think?" He said "I'm not out of line. A lot of these guys in here, if it wasn't for George, they wouldn't even be in business. I know how it is". One of the other guys said "You're making a big mistake". We played cards and no one said anything else about it.

The next day, I'm in my place in Charlottesville. In walks the VIP boy. He asked to see me. I went out and said "What can I do for you?" He said "I just wanted to apologize to you. I got out of hand and I shouldn't have said what I did to you." I could agree with him on that. Basically, word got around to his boss, and he came to see me to tell me in person that he was sorry. He said "Please the next time you see my boss, tell him I apologized to you or I don't have a job anymore." I told him I would tell him. I also told him not to drink so much and to try to keep that attitude in check. He said he would. Then he left. That was that.

Thank you, God, for that time in our lives.

# CHAPTER 24

# Open 24 Hours

In Staunton we were opened for 24 hours. We were packed. There were 2 guys that came in one night, and they had been drinking too much. Every word that came out of their mouth was loud, nasty and vulgar. I walked over to them and said that they would need to lower their voices and watch their mouths if they wanted to eat in here. The one guy said "Alright!" I walked away.

I didn't get very far when not only I could hear, but the people around him could too. He said "Oh F him". I turned around and walked back over and said "You didn't understand what I said. If you're going to use fowl language in here, you'll need to leave and get up, so I can set someone else." He said "Really?" I said, "Yeah, really". He stood up. He had a glass of milk about two thirds full sitting down on the table in front of him. He grabbed the milk and went to hit me with it. I put my arm up. I have a big scar on my arm where he cut me open. Blood started pouring all over. Him and his buddy left for the door. The guy who rang the register said "I'll get them". I said "No, let them go. It's alright." I was bleeding so bad that a girl grabbed a hand towel and wrapped it around my arm. Someone else said that I needed to go to the hospital and they would drive me. So that's what we did. We went to the hospital.

Well, I could take that hand and I could close it, but I couldn't open it. Close it, but not open it. I tried several times. The reason was, he cut all the leaders in my hand that pulls all the fingers open. I thought he had crippled me for sure. The doctor looks at it and said he could fix it. They took "cat gut" and tied my leaders back together because they only I could work was my thumb. Once they got finished with me, I could open it and close it. They did a pretty good job! They wrapped me all up and said to come back and see them in a week or so. I had some problems with it. It hurt. When I went back to see him, he took X-rays and he said there were pieces of glass in there. He had to open it back up, get the glass out, and I'd be okay. So that's what he did.

I got to thinking about that. That boy was one arrogant little cuss. I'll never forget it. I went over one day, I had a van, El Cabrito written all over it, pretty van. I used this to travel to my restaurants. I saw that guy sitting at one of the tables in my restaurant. I said "What in the hell do you think you're doing?" He said "I'm getting ready to eat". I said "Not in here, you're not." I told the waitress to cancel the order. The guy with him said "Look, he's sorry for what he did to you." I said "He's sorry alright". He got convicted and ordered to pay my medical bills, which he never did. I told him he could leave and the guys with him could leave too. I've done so many dumb things in my life, I don't really know what I would have done, but I told them if they didn't get up and leave that I had a pistol in my car and I would shoot him. I went to my car and got it. As I was walking in, with the pistol in my hand, they were all getting up and walking towards the door. I told him not to ever come back in here again or else I would use that pistol on him. We're going they said. I said "Don't you ever come back, because I'll use this pistol on you." They left.

The more I thought about it, the madder I got. So, I called my attorney friend in Waynesboro, and told him what happened. I said I wanted to sue him. He said "He probably doesn't have the money". I said, "Well maybe he'll win the lottery one day, who knows? Sue him." We did. Ten thousand for bodily damage and ten thousand for punitive damage. He could bankrupt the bodily damage, which he did, but he couldn't do anything about that punitive damage. That hung onto him like glue.

Twelve years went by. Twelve years! Katie said someone was on the phone and wanted to talk to me. I knew exactly who it was when he started talking. He had gotten married and had a couple of kids by this time. He couldn't buy a house or do anything because of the judgement out against him. The judgement from what he did to me all those years ago. He went on to tell me that he had gotten hurt on a job and he was going to get about seventeen thousand dollars from it. He wanted to know if he could pay me ten and he'd keep the rest for a down payment on a house. My attorney was supposed to get half of whatever we got out of him. I didn't think I'd get anything ever, so I was okay with just "letting him off the hook" for everything he owed, over the 12 years, all the interest and everything else. My attorney wanted to get the whole seventeen thousand. "To hell with him", he said. I was okay just taking the ten thousand like he had offered. Five thousand for him, five thousand for me. He sounded like a different human being. He was very apologetic He went on to tell me that he had thought about that night so many times. He was truly sorry for everything. My attorney agreed five thousand each would be okay. He paid us, and he was able to get on with his life. He kept the other seven thousand dollars from the money he got out of the accident. The judgement was taken off his records. I got some sort of restitution out of it I guess you could say.

Thank you, God, for getting us through this time in our lives.

# CHAPTER 25

# Moved to Pantops

In 1987 I rented an old night club on Pantops Mountain. It had a lot of work that needed to be done on it. I took my crew up there and we did a fantastic inside job. We bought a few pieces of equipment that I needed. There was some stuff already in there, but I bought a few things. It had an old gravel parking lot. The building could hold 300 or 400 people easy. It had a dining room in the back that could hold 150 people. The room out front could hold another 250 people.

I got a price on what it would cost me to blacktop that parking lot. I don't remember what it was, but it seemed fair enough. Next to the parking lot was a ditch that ran along the side of it. It had a few small locust trees, bushes, beer bottles, whiskey bottles, and all kinds of trash.

I called a friend of mine Walter Burton?? that did excavating. I wanted that ditch cleaned up. All the trees removed, bushes, trash, etc. I wanted him to come after 4:00 in the afternoon, and I told him that whatever he couldn't get done before 6 or 7 at night, to come back in the morning before 10:00. He said "You're getting ready to get me in some kind of trouble aren't you?" I said, "You're getting paid by the hour, so what kind of trouble can you get in?" He agreed to do it for me. He did it and it was perfect. It looked great. The next morning they finished it up and they had even put straw down where they had dug stuff up so that if there was any kind of run off, it would stop it. It wasn't that big of a drop off anyway. Lord have mercy, it looked 100 percent better!

Well, they had just barely gotten off the lot, when all of a sudden here comes a county truck. He pulled up there, rolled out of the truck, him and another guy. I walked out in the parking lot to meet him, and they said "Hey Dave, how are you doing?" I said "I'm trying to mind my own business, how are you doing?" He said "Are you getting smart?" Then he asked me if I had gotten a permit to do the ditch job. I said "What?? I need a permit to clean up around the place?" I knew what was happening. I told him I didn't have one. He said I was supposed to have a permit. I said "Well, what do you recommend I do? Do you want me to have those guys come back with all that trash they picked up and dump it all back down here?" He just looked at me and grinned a little and said, "Naa, I guess you don't need to do that, but if you get written up on it, you'll know why." I said "Yeah, okay". They left.

I never heard anything else from them. Never got anything from the county or anything. That's just the way you had to operate. You couldn't just remodel things without someone hollering down your neck. One day the fire department came up there and wanted to know what kind of paneling was around the place. It was cheap paneling, so I knew it wasn't very good. I had a guy working for me. He was a good worker. In one night, we did everything necessary, to get the paneling "up to code". I put some gloss all over it. The fire marshal came and looked all around and said "Good enough". To be honest with you, if someone would have lit a candle to that thing, it would have gone up in flames. But it never did. I was there a long time and we were busy. It held up just fine. It was a good deal. A good move.

Before we moved to Pantops, I had table toppers on each of the tables that said "Moving to Pantops. No meals tax there". Everyone that came in, they had our back and they were going to follow us up there. Every other year, the county brought back up that meals tax. The people had to vote on it. I had lots of different businesses on my side about this tax. It was just a poor man's tax. If you bought a hot dog at a county store and sat down outside the store, and if you planned on eating it, you had to pay a tax on it. It was just a bunch of off the wall crap!

When it was time to vote again. We beat it and we beat it bad. I made sure to tell people to vote "No to the meals tax". The county said they needed the meals tax for the schools. We kept winning this vote of no meals tax!

In 1996, the year I went out of the restaurant business, they ran that vote again. They had children carrying signs that said "Please help me learn, we need the meals tax". Vote yes to the tax. They had old people sitting at tables handing out flyers that said "Please vote for the meals tax, so that my property taxes don't go up." We lost that year by one vote. One percent.

I went down to the county to a meeting there. I had been there a few times. They knew me well. I was in the crowd. Someone said "Well we have Mr. Flynn here. I know he wanted to say something."

I said, "It took you 10 years, but you finally got it. It's a shame really. 3 more percent on a meal that the poor people don't have. I just wanted to come down here to tell you, that I'm out of the fight. I'm out of the business. I appreciate the respect that I got in the fight and I respect your victory today. I wish you well." They all thanked me. I left.

Thank you, God, for that time in our lives.

# CHAPTER 26

# Mr. Moore

I have to tell you a quick story about leaving across the street from the coliseum, on Emmet Street. I was there for 17 years. I rented it from an old guy who owned the motel there and Lord knows what else he owned. He was wealthy. Tight as he could be. He would rather sleep in the little room he had in that motel and take in the money he made for that hotel than do anything else. That's what I think anyway. He was tight.

People used to ask me, "How in the world do you get a long with him?" His name was Jerry Moore. I'm going to tell you right now, I rented from him, for 17 years. Never had one problem. I had bought cigarette machines that I had purchased for all the restaurants. He had one there at his motel. I put mine in front of his one time. The next thing I knew, he had taken his machine and put his back in front of mine. I ended up talking to him about this. I said "Jerry, this is my foyer, my machine, I have several other of these machines for the other restaurants, and I want one here." He went on to tell me that he had his machine for however long he had where it was. I said "I don't care how long you've had it here, Jerry. I've never asked you for anything you made on it, and I always pay my rent on time." He agreed with me on that. I told him that I wanted his cigarette machine out of there. That if he didn't remove it, I was going to take it out myself and put it out in the parking lot. I told him that I hoped he'd do the right thing. I walked out. Well, he took it out of the foyer, but he put it in his office. When people came in and out of his office, they would see it there. Then out in the foyer was my machine. I couldn't do anything about that, because I wasn't renting that part of the space. I got along with him because I didn't ask him for anything. I knew I wasn't going to get anything from him anyway. I just paid my rent on time, so I got along with him just fine.

Another little story about him. This blows my mind. It blew my mother's mind. Katie's. Everyone who worked in the restaurant. Every year on my mother's birthday, we'd get a cake for her and have coffee and cake for everyone who wanted to participate with us. We told Jerry about this, because he enjoyed coming over in the mornings and getting a cup of coffee from me. A free cup of coffee. He liked the cake and coffee. My mother lived to be almost 92. Jerry died in the early 90's. In his obituary, they had his date of birth. It was the very same day and year that my mother was born. Yet in 17 years, he never once mentioned it. He was just like that. He was a good ol boy. He gave me my "break" when I opened up there 17 years before that. From that point, was how I was able to do everything else I have been telling you about. It all started because of Mr. Moore.

When I look back, I can see the hand of God was on us. Thank you, God, for this time in our lives.

# CHAPTER 27

# Jackson

I RENTED THIS OLD NIGHT CLUB ON PANTOPS MOUNTAIN FROM A GUY named Jackie Jackson. He was a piece of work. One spoiled boy. His grandmother owned that property at one time. She built that building so that he had a place to play his music and what not. She gave him the night club, the property and everything. Spoiled him rotten. Anything he ever wanted, he got. New car, fast car, whatever, he got it. He was something else. He wasn't a good manager of his stuff. When I met with him about renting it, I told him what I would give him for it each month. I told him I would sign a 10-year lease. I was going to fix it up, spend some money on it, put in a new parking lot, remodel the inside of it and everything else. He liked the idea. He went along with it. I can't remember off hand, what the lease was on that thing each month. It wasn't a lot. He had an empty old night club that needed some attention. I gave it the attention it needed and paid the rent. I was supposed to pay the real estate taxes on it each year. They were about 6 or 7 thousand dollars a year. He was behind on them. For about 3 or 4 years he hadn't been paying them.

I was up there for '87, '88, and '89. Westminster Canterbury was getting ready to be built behind it up on the hill. Big project. It would have everything up there. It would be a retirement community, with their own medical staff and everything. It was a big operation. You can look that up and see what an operation that was, if you're so inclined to do so.

Well, they wanted to come up through the property I was renting out, and use that for their entrance to the retirement center. Jackie's attorney got ahold of me and wanted to work out a deal with me. They wanted to see if these people could go up there and use that property. I agreed to meet with them. I saw the plans. They would come right up beside the building. They might have left about 6 parking places on the one side of the parking lot and maybe just as much on the front as well. I had a lot of parking in the front! I didn't want to lose that! They wanted to grade the space in the back so that I wouldn't lose any parking, but it would be back there and no longer in the front. I said that the greatest advertising that I had, was the people parked out in front of the restaurant, so that everyone driving by, could see all the spaces full, right there in front of the building. You can see that from the highway.

The attorney for Westminster Canterbury, was involved in this situation as well. He said, "This is progress Dave. This is improvement". He told me I had to go along with it.

I said to Jackie's attorney, "I'm smart enough to know that I've got a lot of problems." There were a lot of people sitting around that table that day who were involved in the changing of that whole area. It was progress coming alright. The Worrell Farm was getting ready to be all kinds of things. Banks, office buildings, etc. Lots and lots of progress was right. It was coming whether I was ready or not.

I had gas that we used for the cooking. It came from under the road "250". I had water from up on the hill behind me, and I had a sewer system that went off to the farm across the road. I knew that I had a lot of problems coming. I still had 8 years on my lease, and I didn't want that road coming up through that property! I let them all know this. Then I left.

They got all their heads together. The big farm was going to cut the septic system off. It was in the writing many years earlier, that unless something better came along, they couldn't do that. I had that right. So, I went to see one of the big developers, and tried to plead my case. He told me that I didn't have anything better in mind. Between all the developers, the farm, the retirement center people, they had it all "fixed up." They were going to put the "squeeze on me". My attorney, "Bosley", who I used for many years, he got with me and we were supposed to try to work something out. He tried to tell me that I may get some money out of the deal, get my parking lot improved, replaced, etc. He asked me to think about it. I told him that I had thought about it and I didn't like anything about it! I didn't want the road coming through there. It was just that simple.

Not too long after that, I got a letter from Jackie's attorney, saying that they were going to take possession of the property in 60 days because I was failing to "meet my obligations" according to what the lease was. The argument was that I hadn't paid the real estate tax. Well, I paid it all the time. But I hadn't paid it that year because I hadn't received a copy of the bill. I went down to the office building, figured out how much the bill was, I paid it. I told my attorney that I had paid it. Everything was up to date. Bosley told me that they were determined to get me out of there. I told him that it wasn't going to happen!

Then they all got ahold of me, all the ring leaders of this progress process, and they wanted to try to work out a deal. I agreed to this. They said they wanted to talk about the water and the sewer issue.

I had a table that would hold about 12 people. I had a glass of water for each person sitting at each spot. They all came. Out comes the map about the road they wanted to put in by the restaurant. Then Jackie's attorney brought up my failure to pay the real estate taxes. Lord have mercy! My Adam's apple hung up in my throat. I couldn't hardly speak. I got up and walked away from the table. I had to get my composure. I went back. I said "Sir, Dave Flynn, has never crooked, or cheated, or has been delinquent on anything. I have leased property all over the place. I have references from all over the place saying that I pay my rent, on time. He said "It's okay, we are willing to forgive that, if you are willing to let us put in an entrance on this property." I took my fist and hit the table so hard, that water went everywhere. They were still trying to put that road up through that property and I didn't want them to! I had everyone against me. People got up and started backing away from the table. I said "Let me tell you something sir, and I'm going to tell the rest of you gentlemen too, I apologize to you, because I know you are depending on Jackie's attorney to get this all straightened out for you, but this isn't going to happen." I told them to get the heck out and go talk in the parking lot if they had to. To do whatever they wanted. I didn't care if I had to go to court. I didn't care if they were going to cut off my water or my septic, I didn't care. I told them that I had enough income that I could go to court. Then I told Jackie's attorney as I pointed to Jackie, that "He could take that low life with him, and that I never wanted to see him again, except for what he had the right to do as a landlord to come in and inspect the premises." I said I wanted him to call me first, to give me a days' notice, and I'd meet with him, but that as far as anything else was concerned, I was done with him. I told him to leave. He left. Everyone left, and went into the parking lot. Bosely, my attorney, came back in to talk with me. Everyone else was getting in their vehicles and leaving. He said "Dave, I think you need to calm down. I think you can get a nice piece of money out of this if you go along with it." I said "What do you mean about a nice piece of money? Are you talking, 20 thousand, 40 thousand, heck, I wouldn't take 100 thousand dollars and have them do what they are trying to do to me. I don't want that road going up through there! It's just not going to happen. Period".

Bosley went on to tell me that he wasn't sure I'd get that much money. I told Bosley that I wanted him to go to Jackie's attorney's office and to tell him that I needed a letter stating that the real estate taxes were no longer an issue. I wanted to talk with him about the gas, the water, and the sewer. I didn't want to talk to him about anything else. Bosley went to talk with him. For whatever it's worth, a few days later I got a letter from him. The hope was that we could work together in the future and that the delinquency was no longer an issue. It was never an issue to begin with!!

Well, Westminster Canterbury found another way to go up in there. They developed that whole mountain. They put in an entrance and a gate and everything. Lord knows how much money they spent on it all.

Jackie got it in his head that he was just going to sell the property. He wanted 669 thousand dollars or something for it. Well in accordance to the lease, which I had, the real estate agent wasn't going to get more than 400 thousand something for it. They wanted to put a sign up on the property. For sale. I said, "Nope. People don't know if they are buying the land or the restaurant. No sign."

Jackie said he'd drop the price to 650 thousand. I laughed. No commercial real estate company was going to spend that kind of money on a property that wasn't making that kind of a return. I still had 8 years on my lease with the option to renew. He asked if I would be interested in buying it. I said, "I might be." I got ahold of 3 different banks. It was only worth about

400 thousand in accordance to the lease. I had the lease. I wanted to offer them 500 thousand. I thought it would appraise for over 700 thousand. All three banks agreed. For a 20-year term mortgage, I got a heck of a deal because I went to church with the guy who worked at one of the banks. That was a whole other back and forth story. 2 of the banks were trying to out do each other. I went with the best deal out of the 3 banks.

I was told that Jackie wouldn't take what I was going to offer him. I said "That's the offer". I was told he needed 550 thousand dollars to help pay off another property. I said I'd buy the property for the 500 thousand and loan him the other 50 thousand so he could pay off what he needed to pay off. After a few back-and-forth conversations with him, they ended up going with the 500 thousand dollar offer I first had agreed to. He didn't want to have a loan out with me and figured he'd get the money another way. I told their realtor, that I already had a bank willing to give me the loan. The bank appraised the property for 720 thousand dollars. 220 thousand dollars more than what I was paying for it. The bank wanted to charge me an insurance fee for the loan. I told them that we hadn't talked about that. I already had insurance on everything else I was paying on and owned.

When it came time for Jackie Jackson to get his check, I wanted to be the one to hand it to him personally. I told him that I was giving him 100 thousand dollars more than what the lease said it was worth. He said he could have sold it for more. I said "That's beside the point". I told him that I hoped he had learned a lesson in this whole thing. That if you treat people right, they will treat you right in return. I told him that I hoped he gets his life straightened out and wished him the best. Gave him the check, and put my hand out to shake it. He shook my hand in return. Then he and his girlfriend, who had come in with him, left. That's how I was able to get that property on Pantops Mountain. I paid off that 20-year mortgage in 2009 or 2010. I don't remember exactly. It was nice to pay that last payment on it! After that, I decided it was time to get out of there. The kids were not interested in the restaurant business. This would lead me into the next chapter of this story.

Thank you, God, for that time in our lives.

# CHAPTER 28

# Pancake Franchise

After the loan had been paid off, at the Pantops location, I decided it was time to move on. The kids did not want to take over the restaurant business.

I auctioned the equipment off in the place and it was really good turnout. I decided I could rent the property and make just as much money off the rent as I was making in the business. There were these people from Richmond and they wanted to rent the space from me. They had a chain of pancake restaurants. They were a good company. They had a good background on it. They made me a good offer and after discussing it with Katie, we decided that is what we were going to do.

They remodeled the whole property. They put in new bathrooms and redid the dining room area, kitchen, everything. They spent a lot of money. They were good tenants. They were there for 8 years or better. They ended up having to get out because they were not doing so well in the other locations they had elsewhere. They decided to move on. For the remainder of the lease, they owed me about 80 thousand dollars. They agreed to leave me the equipment in the business and they were going to make me the 3rd deed of trust on a piece of property in Goochland to cover the rest. It was questionable if I'd ever get it, because I was the 3rd deed, but I agreed to do that.

I looked for another tenant. I knew a guy really well who had been in the restaurant business for years. He and his wife wanted to continue with a breakfast place there. They were going to keep the equipment there and give me 25 thousand dollars for it and if they agreed to stay after a few years, they would give me 50 thousand more. The rent was pretty expensive. They ended up getting behind. They were not doing well anymore. I had to get him out. He owed me about 40 thousand dollars. I couldn't get anything out of the trust he had. I needed another tenant. At this point I was feeling like I should just sell the property.

It was tax assessed at a little over 2 million dollars. Westminster Canterbury was interested in looking into this. They already had the massive operation on the hill behind it and spent millions of dollars up there. They still wanted a better entrance that would come up through the property of mine. If they bought it, it would be theirs. The county wanted a road to go up between the property and a visitor center that they were talking about putting in. This never did pan out. The deal fell through.

You've got a handful of people in the planning department probably making about 40 or 50 thousand dollars a year, telling people like me, with a 2-million-dollar piece of property, what to do and how it's going to be. Most of the time when dealing with the county, people just give up, because it's so much crap involved and the county knows this. It's not right. It wasn't just that they were doing everything the legal way, they were doing what they wanted to do, and that was that. This ended up being a 3-year battle with the county. Amazing!

There was a bank in Pennsylvania that was interested in the property but there wasn't going to be enough room for a drive through window. Well a bank without a drive through window is ridiculous. That was another opportunity for me to sell the property that went south.

Our son Corven, was in real estate. He was talking to some people from Chick fil A. They were interested in it. I ended up getting rid of everything. I got out of the restaurant business.

It was time for the guy that rented the Dairy Queen property from me in Fredericksburg, to buy the property from me, if he wanted it. He wanted to buy it. I told him he could have it for 10 percent less of whatever it was tax assessed for. I got about 400 thousand dollars out of it. I still owed a couple thousand dollars on that loan. I paid it off and I had about 200 thousand dollars to reinvest in something else. This takes me into another part of the story.

Thank you, God, for this time in our lives.

# CHAPTER 29

# Gate Plaza

I sold that property in Fredericksburg, so I needed to find a property to invest that money in. I didn't want to pay taxes on the capital gain.

There was a property by Food Lion down at Lake Monticello that was for sale. It was raw land. It had a big gully in the back. It was a little less than 4 acres. The people who owned the property lived in North Carolina. They wanted 185 thousand dollars for it. That pretty much took care of the 200 thousand dollars I had to do something with.

I talked with Corven about this. I told him that I thought it would be a good buy. That we could get in some dirt and flatten it out. Come to find out, Corven and my son in law, Joe, thought the same thing. They had already put in an offer on it. They offered 160 thousand dollars for it. I was thinking that I could get some dirt from the guy who had developed some land around the area, and use that to build up this land to where it was useable. I asked Corven if he wanted to partner with me and just go ahead and offer them full price for this land. Corven said he would talk with Joe. At one point the boys made a comment that if they went along with this, they knew that, "it would be the way I wanted things to go." I laughed and said "Not necessarily". I was willing to talk about things but I thought I had a pretty good idea on how to develop the land.

We decided to go look at the property. It would take a lot of work and dirt but we could see the potential. We agreed to make an offer. I would own 50 percent of this property and Joe and Corven would each own 25 percent. It wasn't a bad idea. We offered them the full price of 185 thousand dollars. There were some deed restrictions on it. You couldn't put in a grocery store of any type that would compete with Food Lion. That made sense. There was one other problem. Someone else had made them a little bit better of an offer than ours. They had some contingencies on that offer though, and our offer didn't have those. We had offered them full price and could close in 30 days. I told them that I had been in business a long time and when I make a deal with someone, it's a deal. I felt frustrated that I was being put in this situation and asked how much more was the other offer. They couldn't tell me that. I asked if I was in a bidding war and reminded them that I could close in 30 days with no contingencies. They ended up agreeing and said they would sell it to us. They drew up the paperwork for Joe, Corven, and myself. Now we had 4 acres of land that couldn't be developed the way that it currently was.

In the deed, there were some restrictions about the parking lot. There would be common area parking for both Food Lion and our shopping center to be built. Everything had to be approved. This was a process. The first thing we did was talk to the restaurant people that was in the area. Told them that we wanted to develop the shopping center by Food Lion. Build them a free-standing building that they could help design. They needed more space anyway, and they loved the idea.

Joe, Corven, and I got together to get this built. I had a license that I could build anything in Virginia. We got the subs together and everything we needed to get the building up. In the meantime, I went to meet with the guy who owned the shopping center across the road. He had a big mound of dirt that I was interested in moving across the street. I told him it wouldn't cost him anything, I just wanted the dirt. I would move it at our expense. He agreed to it.

We got the dump trucks. We got a guy in there to load the trucks. We got the inspector out there to check and test every time we built up the dirt. We had a loader, a dozer, a roller, all kinds of equipment up there. It took 1600 loads of dirt to build up that property to where it was a beautiful piece of property.

During this process, we were working day and night. We had rented some construction lights that came in on a trailer, so that the guys could work around the clock to get this done. Lights were shining on the whole thing. This went on for 3 or 4 nights, maybe a little more. One night, the county Sherriff come up and wanted to know who was in charge of this operation. I told him I was close to it anyway, because I was one of the partners in it. He went on to say that the people at the Lake were complaining about all the noise at night. They could not sleep with all the beep beeping of the dump trucks when they backed up. I asked what he recommended us to do. He said we should stop at midnight and then start again in the morning around 7 AM. We lost a few hours of working time because of this, but we agreed to comply. Our crew finished up around 11:00 each night so that they were quiet and done by midnight each night. They came back around 7 in the morning and started again. That went on pretty well for a while.

In order to bring the dirt over, you had to get an okay from the state. This was another process. They said it would take 2 to 3 weeks to get approved.

I said "2 or 3 weeks?? We could have that done and moved before then. The dirt needs to be moved and taken care of." He knew this and I knew this. I explained that we were just moving the dirt from one side of the road to the other. He told me to give him a day and he'd get me a permit to get this done. Within 2 days, I had the permit. So here we were, complying about the noise issue, losing 6- or 7-hours' worth of work, when all of a sudden the next complaint came.

The department for the state came to us saying that the dirt was causing a problem for the people at the Lake driving their cars over the road. There was too much dust on the road from hauling all that dirt across. I told him I'd take care of that. We'd get a broom on a tractor and brush it off. Every day. We did this and the people still complained. They wanted me to wet down the road each night. I said, "So they would rather go through mud than dust?" The guy in charge said, "No, you need to hose it down good, dust it off, and it shouldn't be much of either." We agreed to do this. We had a water truck in there to hose it off. The tractor to sweep the road. A whole outfit for the project. This went fine. We got that property built up in there. There was still quite a holler behind it, but everything got okayed as far as building on it goes. We got the restaurant built. Then we started on the other building where we had several other tenants. We also had another section with several other places for shops. We ended up having a handful of really, wonderful tenants over the years. One lady has been there for over 17 years. They were a handful of tenants that didn't last long. A few that had their own issues, or didn't want to pay what I was asking per square foot. Overall, we've been very happy with the shopping center and our tenants. Some are even still there to this very day! My, how the time flys by. It seems like it was just yesterday we built that place up. The pharmacy is still there and is doing well. The pet store has been around since the very beginning.

I look back and see God's hand was in the process with us during the whole thing. It's been over 20 years at this point. We're still renting out the shops and still thankful for our tenants.

Thank you, God, for this time in our lives.

# CHAPTER 30

# Chick-fil-A

After a 3-year battle with the county of Albemarle, and after having 2 good deals fall though, because the county would not okay anything; We finally found something that could work. Corven, our son, found a company named Chick-fil-A who was interested in making a deal.

The county drove me nuts about this situation. I never could get an appointment with the head guy. I always had to deal with someone under him. It had me a nervous wreck for 3 years. To this day it still boggles my mind how they operate up there.

Chick-fil-A was wonderful to work with. There could not be a better organization. Chick-fil-A offered me 33 thousand dollars for the equipment that I had in the old restaurant. That helped to recover the 40 thousand that the last tenant had left me with.

The guy who owned some land next to my property, wanted to sell his ½ acre lot. 263 thousand dollars. I could not sell my piece because the government would take tons of it for capital gain. I was too old, and too worn out, to try to figure out what to do with that money. What it boiled down to, was that I was better off keeping that property. I told Chick-fil-A that I would lease the land to them. We had come to a good agreement on that. They wanted me to buy the ½ acre lot next to me. So, I would have 4 acres of land instead of 3 ½. I did not want to do that. This went back and forth for a bit. Finally, Chick-fil-A decided to buy the half acre lot. They ended up deeding it to me, so that the property was 4 acres and no longer 2 separate deeds. The county did not want it to be 2 separate deeds anymore. Something about the half acre lot being too small.

We all went through a lot of run around with the county, but things started to line up slowly. The county wanted a road put in the back of the property. After much push back and battling, the road went in. The county also was giving Chick-fil-A a hard time because they wanted to put in a 2-lane drive through window system up there. I attended a meeting one day with the county about this. 2 guys came from the Atlanta main office, to show their presentation about the 2-lane drive through and how successful it was. They said that within a minute of ordering, you could pick up your order. They had other locations, and this had proved to be true. At one point during the meeting, one of the guys from the county gave his push back. I was so fed up and frustrated with these types of people, I almost came out of my seat. Katie was next to me. She grabbed my leg and told me to calm down. I ended up needing to go out in the hall for a few minutes. I had just about had enough of this.

The guys from Chick-fil-A kept their cool the whole time and they told me later that everything would be okay. They knew what the county wanted and they knew how to work with these types of people.

Chick-fil-A opened in November of 2016 or 2017 I cannot remember exactly when. They are always busy. That double drive thru really helped them out. Even during the pandemic, they were still busy. I do not think they hardly dropped at all during that time. I think it is because of that double drive thru window. Most people were afraid to get out and go anywhere in 2020. Fast food places were still doing drive thru though, and Chick-fil-A had not one, but two lanes. What a smart operation!

One of the smartest things I have ever done, was make this deal with Chick-fil-A. They are an excellent tenant. They got a land lease and they pay it like clockwork. I was not sure how they could spend all the money they spent getting the building up, buying the other lot, all the expenses they had, and hope to make that money back. They told me, "We'll get it all back in 5 years". As busy as they are, I have no doubt in my mind that is what they have done.

The manager of the Pantops location, is a heck of a nice guy. Sweet family. Wife and a few kids. I joked with him, that once he opened, all that nice dark hair he had, would turn grey. He laughed. He is still running that location to this day. They know how to operate. They are a good Christian organization. They close every Sunday. You cannot do any better than that.

Long story short, I am so glad I did what I did. It sure helps me now, especially with the small social security check I get.

Thank you, God, for this time in our lives.

# Conclusion

If you have gotten this far, then God willing, you have read my stories. Hopefully you can find humor in some of it. I hope you can find some amazement as well. I desire for you, to understand that you will always have partners in your life. Some you are born with, and some you choose. Thank you for sticking with me on this journey. God bless you! I hope that you choose for yourself the greatest partner, God. Our creator of everything. I am so thankful that God stuck with me throughout all this stuff in my life. If I did not have the Lord, I would not be here today.

I also want to acknowledge that fact, that God blessed me with the greatest wife there is. Katie has put up with me through thick and thin. I really do not deserve to have such a wonderful wife, but our Lord is gracious, and He knew that I would need someone like Katie, to stand by me. For better or worse, for richer or poorer; Through all the ups and the downs, Katie was patient with me. She really was the backbone of the whole operation. She is the glue that held things together when I might be tearing everything apart.

You know they say, behind every good man, is an even better woman. Katie is that woman. I love Katie so much and I am thankful to have her in my life. I am pretty sure that no other woman would have put up with the stuff Katie did. We have been married for 60 years. I do not know how one man could be this blessed, but I was, I am, and I'm thankful for it.

I want to say thank you to our three amazing kids, Corven, Breck, and Cyndra. Thank you for putting up with me as well. Thank you, to our wonderful grandkids. Aaron, Kinzie, Josiah, and Jeremiah. They all, are the loves of my life. We also have a great grandchild. Callan. I am truly blessed. Thank you, Lord, for my family! What a wonderful partnership I have.

I want to refer back to Chapter 4, where I mentioned a woman with child knocking on my door. 19 years later, I met this child, Gina. Our family welcomed her into our lives. Gina married, and had 2 children, Leann, and Mark. She has 2 grandchildren, Georgia, and Lincoln. Gina died in 2022.

I want to say thank you to my daughter in law, Lisa Flynn, who helped videotape my stories over a three-year span. She was patient with me and she knew how to use the technology that this old hillbilly did not understand. If it was not for her, this book would not have been possible. Thank you, Lisa.

I want to say thank you, to Kati Forman. I know God brought her into our lives to help us complete this project. She previewed all those videos, 35 of them to be exact. She listened to my words, and put them down on paper for me. She typed this whole thing. Thank you, Kati.

This might sound selfish of me, but I wanted my story to be down on paper so that my kids, grandkids, and great grandkids, could remember me when I am gone. Gone but not forgotten. I want my stories to live on with them. I pray for them to remember the life I had. I pray they choose wisely, their partners. I pray they choose God for themselves.

I want to say thank you to everyone in my life who has worked for me, under me, and with me. Thank you for your partnership. I could not have done what I have done without your help.

I also want to say, that I am not anti-government. I think we live in the best country in the world. I do think it would be better if the government was not so big, if they would spend less money, and possibly give us a chance for more.

Thank you, and Amen

# Epilogue

It has been six months since I started on this journey with the Flynn's. I came into this situation, thinking I was just doing Dave a favor. Little did I know, God would use this story for my own healing journey at the same time.

I have laughed out loud while typing up Dave's words. I have also cried many tears. I have thought long and hard about some of the things he has said. I have been taken back to when I was a child, remembering how Pantops Mountain first looked when my parents moved here in 1993. It is interesting to hear the "behind the scenes" stories Dave went through. All the progress that happened to make it look like the hustling, bustling place it is today.

I went down memory lane as Dave talked about the plaza at Lake Monticello. I will never go into that shopping center again, without thinking about how many dump trucks of dirt, it took to build that place up to where it is to this day. David Flynn's handiwork is all over that shopping center. I stand amazed.

One of our favorite places to eat is Chick-fil-A. Every time I sit in that 2-lane drive through, I smile to myself, knowing that on that same piece of land, once stood another place. Another memory. Another season of life. Bittersweet. Time and change and progress. One thing is for sure, nothing ever stays the same. Nothing but our God. He is constant. The same, yesterday, today, and tomorrow.

I have prayed for this family along this journey. Prayed for Dave and his dad. Prayed for the different people that have touched these stories for better and worse. I have thanked God for this opportunity to be just a tiny little part of their lives, for "such a time as this." I feel blessed.

I am both humbled and honored at how amazing our God is. How He is always looking out for our good. Roman's 8:28, in the New King James Version says,

*"And we know that all things work together for good to those who love God, to those who are the called according to His purpose."*

I think it is fair to say, that verse sums up David Flynn's life.

This is a reminder to me, as the reader of the Flynn's story, that God was and is, a partner in their lives.

God is not done with this story yet. He is not done with any of us. We are all works in progress. All of us make mistakes. Every one of us, falls short. Praise God, that He loves us anyway. The bible says that, "love covers a multitude of sins." It also says in, John 3:16. "For God so loved the world that He gave His only begotten Son, that whoever believes in Him should not perish but have everlasting life." We are all God's children. One big family. Choose for yourself whom you will serve.

As for me and my household, we will serve the Lord.

Thank you, God, for this time in our lives.

With appreciation,

Kati

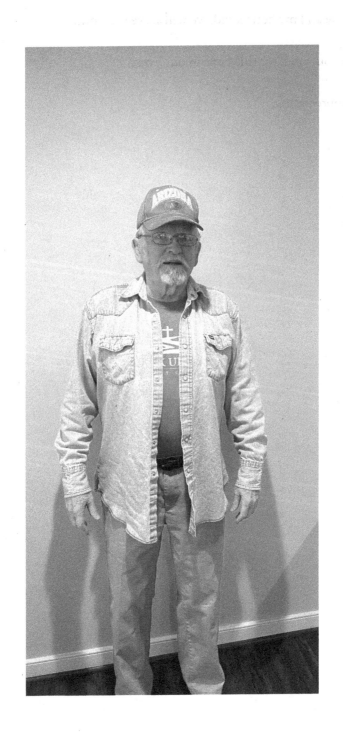

**S.M.A.R.T.**

Sensible, Modest And Reasonable Taxes

**Dave Flynn**
**Public Relations Director**

PO Box 5849
Charlottesville, VA 22905

804-963-7780